BIG BEN

LAWRENCE SCANLAN

Cover photo by Ellen Tofflemire

Inset photo by Jayne Huddleston

Scholastic Canada Ltd.

Scholastic Canada Ltd.
175 Hillmount Road, Markham, Ontario L6C 1Z7

Scholastic Inc.
555 Broadway, New York, NY 10012, USA

Scholastic Australia Pty Limited
PO Box 579, Gosford, NSW 2250, Australia

Scholastic New Zealand Limited
Private Bag 94407, Greenmount,
Auckland, New Zealand

Scholastic Ltd.
Villiers House, Clarendon Avenue, Leamington Spa,
Warwickshire CV32 5PR, UK

Designed by Yüksel Hassan.

Canadian Cataloguing in Publication Data

Scanlan, Lawrence
  Big Ben

ISBN 0-590-24187-7

1. Big Ben (Horse) - Juvenile literature.
2. Show jumping (Horses) - Canada - Biography - Juvenile literature.
I. Title.

SF295.565.B583 1994   j798.25   C94-930676-2

10 9 8 7 6 5   Printed in Canada   9 / 9 012 / 0

Acknowledgements

I owe thanks to Diane Kerner for her thoughtful editing, to Jayne Huddleston for sharing her expertise, to Harry van Hooydonk for all the Belgian material, to Sandi Patterson for her insight into Big Ben's character and to Ian Millar who had the good sense to buy the horse and the skill to make him a champion.

Numerous readers, among them the Carpenters (Reeves, Claudine and David), Sarah Jagger, Marnie Young, Donna Kennedy-Berry at Millar Brooke Farm and the folks at Wilmarny Farm, read the manuscript and offered helpful comments. Special thanks to Jan Whitford, my agent, for all her good work, and to my family, Ulrike Bender and Kurt Scanlan, who manage to nurture both the author and his projects, including this one.

Finally, bran muffins and carrots galore to Big Ben, the chestnut horse whose greatness I felt so compelled to chronicle.

To my son Kurt

Contents

Big Ben gets the distinctive pat that Ian Millar reserves for him: the right hand on the horse's left side. (Photo by Jayne Huddleston)

1

The Mighty Ben

So distinctive is this horse that if you have seen him perform, even just once, you keep the memory of him. Ears pricked forward. Tail and head held high with excitement. The socks on his rear legs a white blur. Eating up turf with that long and seemingly effortless stride of his. Moving quickly without seeming to. Turning in the corners like a cat. Flying up and over every jump, even the most difficult combination jumps. His rider's quiet hands on him.

Then, at the end, the rider's distinctive pat: right

hand crossing over to the left side of the horse's neck. And, often as not, a ribbon, followed by a victory gallop around the show ring.

Big Ben.

World Cup champion in 1988 and 1989. Twice winner of the Spruce Meadows Masters grand prix — the most hotly contested show jumping prize in the world. Gold medalist twice at the Pan American Games in 1987. Winner of more than fifty grand prix victories all over the world through the 1980s and 1990s. A horse the insurance companies valued at $1 million.

The way in which horse and rider came together more than a decade ago reads like a fairy tale. What were the odds that gifted Canadian rider Ian Millar would find this oversized Belgian warmblood horse an ocean away and make him into a legend?

This fairy tale might have had a far darker ending. The hero of our story is a horse, a living breathing animal — not a fictional creation like Black Beauty. But Big Ben's life reads like fiction, full of twists and turns and calamity. On three separate occasions, it seemed the story would end tragically. He bounced back every time. He leaves you breathless.

Big Ben's physical stature alone is something you never quite get used to. You look again, and again. One hundred seventy three centimetres tall at the shoulders. Some 240 centimetres tall at the ears. You see him in his stall and you think, *I would need a*

Although Ian Millar is a tall man, Big Ben towers over him.
(Photo by Jayne Huddleston)

ladder to get on him. He holds his head high, which makes him even more imposing, more regal. He is a solid 650 kilos of professional horse.

His quirky character amuses and intrigues you: the way he prefers the company of children to that of adults, bran muffins to almost anything, green apples over red. The way he pouts in his stall when his personal groom, Sandi Patterson, is not there. And the fuss he creates if he sees the horse van going to a competition without him.

His great accomplishments in the show ring have filled tack rooms with ribbons, trophies, victory blankets, not to mention more than $1.5 million in prize money. But prizes hardly begin to tell the story of Big Ben.

★ ★ ★

This world-famous horse spends most of his time in Ontario, at Millar Brooke Farm.

Millar Brooke is a horse farm. When you close the barn's Dutch door behind you, you enter the world of horses and horse smells: the sweet sweaty must of horse blankets, the aroma of good hay, the breath of cedar shavings in sawdust. And despite all the mucking out of stalls and the fussiness that rules this white barn with the black tin roof, there is just a hint of that *other* scent — horse manure. The scent is old and familiar, as reliable as a good friend.

Have you ever groomed a horse as the sun beamed through the stall window? The dust flies off the horse's back, hangs in the sunbeam, then drifts lazily downward. It drifts and circles back, in fact, to where it came from. Which is why grooming never ends. Just as likely, the horse dust finds your nostrils, clothes and riding boots. It lingers on you, like a fond memory. You remember for a time that ride. How it all came together, or fell apart.

Those with a special feeling for horses believe that to ride a horse is to get a leg up on the world, that a horse barn is a haven. Or is it heaven?

The vitality of Millar Brooke Farm comes partly from the to-ing and fro-ing of grooms and vets and blacksmiths, partly from the horses themselves. And no ordinary horses either. These are champions and champions-in-the-making. The coats always shine. The hooves are always oiled. The nameplates on the stalls are made of brass. Lonesome Dove. Future Vision. And over in that north-facing stall, Big Ben.

His rider, Ian Donald Millar, is a champion too. He calls the star of his stable "the mighty Ben." The partnership of this horse and this rider is nothing short of equestrian magic. In the show ring, they are recognized instantly: the tall, lanky rider in blazer and glasses, the huge liver chestnut horse with the proud step and the red maple leaf on his white saddle pad. He always generates a little buzz of anticipation. The Ian Millar/Big Ben combination is *supposed* to win, and for a long, long time they have done just that.

As you follow the chronicle of Big Ben's remarkable life, you begin to understand his character. Because he is horse and you are human, there is much you cannot know. But this much is certain: You do not forget Big Ben, this horse with the white blaze now fading to grey. He jumps so high and with such grace that you would swear the horse had wings.

Nostrils flaring, mane flying, Big Ben vaults an obstacle with Ian Millar on board. (Photo by Todd Korol)

2

Lightning Strikes Twice

January 3, 1991. A cold grey day was dawning at Millar Brooke Farm. Circling in his stall and pawing the ground with his hooves was a tall chestnut horse. Sandi Patterson, the horse's one and only groom since 1987 and his best friend in the world, looked in his stall as she does every morning at 7:00 A.M. and she did not like what she saw.

Sandi is a tiny woman with a round face and pleasant features. She is in her mid-thirties, but seems much younger. Her short, blondish hair rolls in tight little waves from left to right across her head. She calls the horse she dearly loves "Bennie." It seems a proper name for a pony, not a giant horse. But given the affection between this horse and this woman, "Bennie" fits like a slipper.

When she walks him on a lead rope — Sandi taking two choppy steps to Big Ben's one — the contrast is vivid. The horse seems even bigger, the groom even smaller. They are an odd couple, but they are as close as a horse and a human can get.

Sandi is known for her warmth and generosity, for finding time to be kind even in times of intense pressure. But the most remarkable thing about Sandi — the thing that everyone marvels at — is her devotion to Big Ben. It knows no bounds. It is hard for many people to understand. And it effectively rules out a normal social life and normal working hours.

Sandi understands Big Ben as no one else does, and when she worries about him her face takes on a pinched look. The anguish shows in her eyes, in the tightness of her mouth, as it did on that cold winter morning.

Big Ben had ignored his morning grain, and that was not normal. Sandi called the veterinarian, Dr. John Atack, who came running. Along with his wife, Dr. Linda Berthiaume, he operates an equine clinic at Millar Brooke Farm. His office is just across the gravel parking lot, close enough to afford a view of Big Ben's stall window.

Best friends — Big Ben and groom Sandi Patterson. (Tampa Tribune
photo)

Dr. Atack is thin and wiry, built like a reed. He often wears blue jeans and a baseball cap. His manner is loose and casual. You might take him for a farm hand or a truck driver. But you would be wrong. He is a horse vet, and a fine one. He examined Ben while Sandi watched and longed for an encouraging word.

Say he's fine. Tell me not to worry. Everything will be OK.

"I don't like the looks of it," Dr. Atack told Sandi, and her heart sank like a stone in water.

Sandi led the horse to the indoor arena. Clearly uncomfortable, Big Ben pawed the ground, dug holes and then rolled over. He kept looking back at his side. Normally, when turned out in the ring each morning, he has a pleasant roll, canters a bit and then reclines where the low eastern sun strikes the ground. But this morning he was trying to shake off pain that would not be shaken off.

The bowels of a horse are like a thirty-metre-long garden hose, and whatever the horse eats must pass through that jumble. A blockage can cause stabbing pain, and often death. Horse people call it colic and they live in fear of it.

Big Ben had suffered a gruesome attack of colic in Florida not ten months before. It had been one of the worst moments of Sandi's life. That whole nightmare — the three hours of surgery, the cold fear that his time in the ring, and perhaps even his life, had come to an end — was something Sandi had tried to put behind her.

They say lightning never strikes twice in the same place. But this was not lightning, this was *colic*. The word hit her like a slap. Colic is the number one killer of horses.

I can't believe this is happening. Panic came at Sandi in waves. The thought of surgery for any horse at Millar Brooke was hard to bear. But this was Ben, her Bennie. Sandi wanted that sick feeling in the pit of her stomach to go away.

Ian Millar and his wife, Lynn, were in New York State looking at horses to buy. Around 9:30 that morning, Sandi got Ian on the telephone and broke the news.

"Let me talk to John," he said grimly. The vet confirmed that Big Ben seemed colicky.

"This is like turning back the clock," Ian told Dr. Atack. There was an edge to his voice. He too could scarcely believe this was happening.

"I know," the vet replied. "Listen, we'll do what we can here. But if he doesn't improve soon, Ian, we'll take him to the clinic at the University of Guelph."

"OK," sighed Ian. "But keep me posted, will you?"

Now he and Lynn faced a ten-hour drive home, worrying every minute of the way. Sometimes the only thing worse than being there is *not* being there.

Sandi said very little as she watched Dr. Atack work on Big Ben, but her mind raced.

Do something, she pleaded with her eyes. *Make it go away.*

Dr. Atack tried for ninety minutes. He did everything he could to clear the blockage. Walking. Fluids. Oils. Nothing worked.

"Come on, Sandi. We have to get him to Guelph," he said finally. Then he called ahead to tell the clinic they were on their way.

Oh no. Not this. Not again.

Quickly, Sandi led Big Ben into one of the smaller horse vans. Along with Dr. Atack and a driver, they set off for the veterinary clinic at the University of Guelph in southwestern Ontario. For the second time in less than a year, surgeons would have to cut into Ben.

On that bitterly cold day, Guelph seemed an eternity away for Sandi. The trip took six and a half hours. In cross-ties (straps snapped into the halter and attached to hooks on both sides), Ben endured his agony with astonishing tolerance. The same spirit that works wonders in the ring was surprising even Dr. Atack, who knows the horse well. The vet gave him a tranquillizer and a painkiller while Sandi stayed with him in the trailer, trying to offer comfort with reassuring words and the touch of her hands.

As the hours passed and the van sped along Highway 401, the pain got steadily worse. Big Ben would try to throw himself down onto the floor of the van, hoping to roll and drive the pain away.

Colic pain has been compared by some vets to the pain that a woman feels at childbirth. Pain to make a human cry out and beg for relief; pain to bring a tough, proud horse to his knees.

Thirty kilometres from Guelph, Sandi hammered on the window and asked the driver to stop. Dr. Atack went into the trailer and gave Big Ben another shot in a last attempt to stop the suffering. For both Sandi and Dr. Atack, who had long marvelled at the horse's dignity, it was a withering experience to watch him brought so low.

By the time the horse van pulled up in front of the large-animal clinic at the University of Guelph, it was early evening.

The clinic's admitting office, red-brick with a unicorn weather vane perched jauntily on its green copper roof, is a bright and welcoming place. Framed photographs of former patients — prized cows and horses — are displayed on the walls. By the door stands a sculpture made of black steel and horse-shoes, depicting a miniature horse and rider. Sandi rushed past it and braked at the counter.

"Please," she said, almost breathless with distress. "Dr. Atack called you. We've got a horse outside with colic. It's really bad."

In minutes, Big Ben was led into a holding area, a vast entryway with a black rubber floor. Sandi took him to a slightly raised section, set off by a metal railing, where he was quickly weighed. If surgery lay ahead, they would need a precise weight in order to calculate how much anaesthesia was needed. Then the horse was brought to an examining room, backed into a sturdy metal stock with bars fore and aft and examined rectally. The news was not encouraging.

The surgeon on call that night was a lanky veterinarian named Ron Trout. He wears glasses, and his neat brown moustache matches his thick head of hair. The surgeon's manner is calm and confident, and he often uses his hands and eyes to emphasize points as he speaks.

"He's got a fairly high heart rate," Dr. Trout told Sandi and Dr. Atack, "and that's an indicator of pain. He's not in bad shape as far as his heart goes but you can see how bloated he is, especially around the flanks. And I could feel that his large intestine is dramatically swollen."

It came to this: without surgery right away, the horse would die.

In minutes, the big gelding was ushered into a stall-sized room. He was eased towards one side, and kept there by a pair of blue padded shutters about thirty centimetres thick. The anaesthetic that followed worked almost instantly. Big Ben wavered, his head lolled, and he dropped heavily to his knees. As attendants slowly opened the shutters, the unconscious horse fell sideways onto a thick mat. He fell, in fact, onto the operating table.

Powered by a hydraulic lifter, the table rose from below and stopped about waist height. Veterinary technicians used a lifter and chains attached to the ceiling to position the horse with his belly up and his legs in the air. They placed metal plates into slots on the table's sides and each end to prevent him from sliding off.

Moving methodically about the small room, they shaved Big Ben's belly and part of his neck. They put white plastic covers over his hooves to reduce the risk of infection. They covered his body with green sheets. And when they were done, they opened the far door and wheeled Big Ben into an operating room almost identical to one in a modern hospital. In green gowns, masks and plastic gloves, Dr. Trout, the anaesthetist and the team began to work on Big Ben.

A tube was inserted in the horse's throat and the anaesthetist — the captain of the surgical team — stayed at his head to monitor the flow of oxygen. Another tube was inserted in his neck so blood pressure could be checked. When all was ready, the technicians began reaching into the trays for retractors, clamps, forceps and scalpels.

Sandi could not bear to look. But neither could she tear herself away. Through a television monitor located in a nearby room, she and Dr. Atack watched the entire operation. She soon lost all sense that this exposed horseflesh was her Ben. His unseeing eyes were wide open. Someone kept putting drops in them to keep them from drying up. Sandi saw those eyes and was chilled by them.

He's still alive, she had to tell herself over and over. *He's still alive.*

There was, of course, method to everything that Dr. Trout was doing. But as he pored over and under the horse's intestines — swollen to balloon size — he looked like someone who had lost something, a set of keys perhaps, inside the body of a living creature.

As the hours passed, Sandi began to pace before the TV monitor. It was as if someone had recorded on film one of her nightmares and she was being made to watch it.

★ ★ ★

With every dark twist in Ben's fortunes, there has always been a little light. This attack of colic was cleanly and simply resolved. Dr. Trout found the blockage where the large colon narrows into the small colon. He injected a salt solution into the hard, doughy mass, gently kneading it and spreading it out. Then he stopped, confident that nature — Big Ben's own horse plumbing — would move it all out later. Had the surgeon been forced to remove the blockage by cutting into the intestine the odds of recovery would have declined, for the chance of infection would have risen.

Within an hour, Big Ben was starting to wake up in recovery — a small room with green padded walls, a red rubber floor embedded with grit to give the

17

patient better footing, and rounded corners to reduce the risk of injury. When he was still unconscious, attendants fitted a blue padded crash helmet on him. The wrap-around headgear with holes cut out around the eyes gave him a sorry look — like a poor knight's charger, or a boxer who has gone too many rounds in the ring. His stomach stuck out crazily from the build-up of gas.

Then the surgical team stepped out of the stall. Along with Sandi, they waited and hoped.

Sandi dared not go in to comfort or calm Big Ben as he slowly regained consciousness. Horses are often violent after surgery. Many racehorses, for example, survive their operations but then panic afterwards when they find themselves unable to stand up. They sometimes open up their stitches or break their legs as they flail about.

Call it good luck, or just plain horse sense, but Big Ben somehow knew better than to thrash. He sat on his haunches like a dog and he stayed that way until he was sure he could stand up. But the horse that finally stood up looked nothing like the one that Sandi knew. In his silly-sad crash helmet, with thick white bandages wrapped completely around him, he looked like a cartoon figure of a tired old war horse.

That night Sandi walked him briefly, and afterwards every hour for fifteen minutes. At least he was moving. The walking seemed to do them both some good. By now it was 3:00 A.M., and Dr. Atack and the driver headed back to Millar Brooke Farm.

Sandi slept that first night in a small corner stall — number 416 — next to Ben's. His stall was, oddly enough, much like his own at Millar Brooke Farm. Sliding wooden door. Silver painted bars. The smell of wood shavings in the air. But like a grim reminder that this was a hospital, not home, a thick plastic intravenous line curled from a spot in his neck up towards the ceiling.

Sandi rarely left him. Eventually, she found a hotel room nearby, but most of the time she was there to keep Big Ben company. No one outside the university was allowed in, of course, but word had spread around the campus that Big Ben was a patient in a

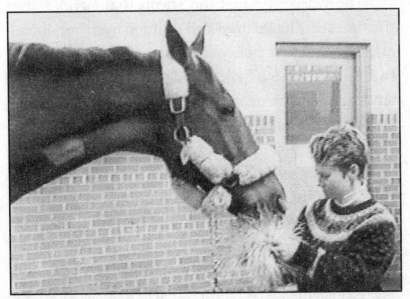

Still wearing a bandage on his neck from the operation, Big Ben gets some hydroponically grown grass from Sandi. (Photo from Millar Brooke Farm videotape)

ward stall at the large-animal clinic. A great many people walked by and took discreet peeks at the famous show jumper.

A few days after the surgery, someone at the clinic took a video of Sandi walking Big Ben. It was done for Ian, to assure him that all was well with his horse. The video shows Ben wearing a thick white lambskin halter, being led on a rope by Sandi. He wears two tan-coloured bandages — a small one at his neck where the intravenous line had been, and a huge one, running almost the entire length and width of his belly, where the surgeons went in. He moves gingerly and looks forlorn. Yet the ears are still forward, still keen.

The video captures the strain that Sandi felt at the time. She looks tired and drained from her ordeal, as if she had just woken from an epic but fitful sleep. But there is also a look of relief and an odd crimped smile on her face as she slowly walks the horse back and forth down a wide hallway. At one point, Sandi and Big Ben tuck into a doorway to let someone pass leading another patient — a Holstein cow. There is no sound on the video, but something makes Sandi laugh. Did the cow moo? Did Big Ben respond?

Then, unrehearsed, a young girl of about eleven enters from the right and shyly hands Sandi a card. The girl seems awed by the presence of Big Ben. She holds her hands together in front and looks at the camera, only occasionally at the horse. Sandi seems

Big Ben examines a
get-well card presented
by a young fan after his
colic surgery at the
University of Guelph
veterinary clinic. (photos
from Millar Brooke
Farm videotape)

genuinely pleased by her gesture. The card, of course, is for Ben.

GET WELL SOON, BIG BEN reads the hand-printed card. It shows a picture of a horse on the front and a big heart in the upper right-hand corner. Sandi shows it to Ben, who looks on politely. Sandi allows herself a laugh.

Hundreds more cards like this one arrived later at the clinic. Some fans even sent bran muffins and carrots.

Back at Millar Brooke Farm, Ian stayed in touch by phone with Sandi. Barring further complications, the horse would live, and Ian was relieved to hear the news. But no one in the horse world believed for a second that Big Ben at the age of fifteen years could endure two colic operations — never mind two within less than a year — and return to form in the show ring.

It was over.

3

The Colt Called Winston

Near the town of Wuustweezel (pronounced Woost-*way*-zl) in northern Belgium is the farm of Jacobus van Hooydonk and Louisa Van Looveren. Antwerp is twenty-five kilometres to the southwest, and the Dutch border is a few kilometres to the north. The countryside is cooled by breezes off the North Sea, or the Noordzee, as the Flemish call it.

At the van Hooydonk farm an unusually tall foal was born on April 20, 1976. A liver chestnut — a deep red-brown colour — he bore a blaze on his forehead, or, more precisely, a star, a stripe and a snip. On his hind legs were white socks.

Jacobus van Hooydonk is a kindly man with large hands and a full head of snow-white hair. During the Second World War, British soldiers had sought shelter at the van Hooydonk family farm, which was later destroyed by bombing. Jacobus's father had built the farm himself in the 1930s, hacking out a place among the heather and fir trees. After the war, the van Hooydonks rebuilt the farm and began breeding horses. Horses and van Hooydonks seemed to go together.

In 1954 Jacobus took over the family farm and in 1968 — at the age of forty-three — he bought his first horse. A string of foals followed. When the new foal came in 1976, he needed a name. For some reason, Jacobus thought of Winston Churchill, the wartime British prime minister. "Churchill was like a rock in a stormy sea," he told his sons.

Further inspiration came from the Belgian warmblood breeding association, which declared that all registered horses born that year must have names beginning with the letter W. So the tall foal with the big head was called Winston.

The big barn where Winston was born is built of red and yellow brick, the colours of a peach, with a corrugated tin roof. It is set very close to the farmhouse. The farm seems modest in size by Canadian standards: a mere eight hectares with a small stand of woods. The land is flat, and right next to the farm is a huge nature preserve called De Kempen. This was home to the horse we now call Big Ben.

The horse's sire was a sixteen-hand stallion, friendly as stallions go, named Etretat (pronounced *Ate*-ra-tah). One hand is four inches (a bit more than ten centimetres), so Etretat was a little more than 1.6 metres tall at the shoulder. He was a three-quarter thoroughbred racehorse, bought by Jacobus's brother Louis in France and stabled nearby at his farm. The grandson of a pure thoroughbred called Enfant Terrible, Etretat would go on to sire more horses than any other stallion in the Belgian stud-book.

Big Ben's mother was a mare named Oekie (pronounced *Oo*-key), a Belgian warmblood and an unusually friendly horse. Jacobus's son Harry remembers her as "the charming lady of the farm." Agreeable to ride. Always gentle in her manner. She passed on to Big Ben her liver chestnut colour and her odd angles.

The strange thing is that Ookie was relatively small — 15.3 hands at most. It seems curious that a little mare and an average-sized stallion would produce such a 17.3-hand giant.

Grand prix riders call horses such as Big Ben "freaks." Riders use the word with affection. Most horses simply cannot or will not leap high fences.

Show jumpers must possess extraordinary power — riders call it "scope" — and just as much courage. Riders hope to spot the freak horse before another rider does, and ride that freak to glory.

Jacobus knew that Winston was a good one. But he could not have foreseen what a horse, what a freak, he had on his hands. Nothing about Oekie, for example, would have told him that. Jacobus was fond of Oekie. The foals always came quickly and easily to her. Jacobus would go out to the barn and check on her at midnight when another foal was coming, but she seemed almost secretive about her births. Jacobus would peek again in the middle of the night. Still no foal. But in the morning, there the foal would be. Jacobus cannot remember, but perhaps Winston was born like that, a gangling young thing, all legs and head, who came in the night. A warm and still-wet newborn who rose up on his legs with the sun to herald the morning.

When he was a year and a half old, the colt was put out in a large field bordered on two sides by a nature preserve. A quiet place that attracts many birds, the preserve is known for its sand dunes, marshland and trees that have grown there for centuries. It is as wild as any place in Belgium.

Winston shared the field with only one other horse, his younger sister Udet, and he stayed there from May until September. Jacobus or one of his two sons, Harry and Daniel, would go out on a bicycle

The van Hooydonk farm at Wuustweezel. At the bottom is the main house, and at the middle left is the horse barn. The tiny horse at the top centre of the photo is Winston. (Photo courtesy Harry van Hooydonk)

every few weeks to check on him, but the horse was uninterested in human contact. Winston seemed to love his solitude.

Getting close to this shy, skittish horse took sugar and gentle coaxing. In October, Jacobus brought him by horse van into the stable for the winter, and Winston gradually got used to people again.

The next spring they turned him out for the season, and again he felt the freedom of his field. The occasional checks took more sugar and patience.

During the winter, Jacobus turned Winston out in the indoor ring to keep him supple and to relieve the boredom of the stall. On one occasion, when the horse was about two and a half years old, Winston did something strange. He began to leap over the 1.3-metre jump set up in the ring. Jacobus had been around horses most of his life, but he had never seen anything like it. There was no rider or trainer to issue the instruction, and Winston had never jumped a fence in his life. But he jumped this one, and not once, but three times without touching the rail. What struck Jacobus was how naturally and playfully the horse jumped. He simply had it in him — the desire to jump.

Jacobus's son Daniel, then about eighteen years old but already the winner of many ribbons at provincial show jumping and dressage competitions, took on the task of saddling and training him. Winston, by

April 1980: Big Ben, still known as Winston, as a four-year-old at the van Hooydonk farm in Belgium.

now a gelding, accepted the saddle much more quickly than Daniel had expected him to. The horse had always been so wary of new things.

During his first dressage lessons, Winston would side-step each time he neared one of the letters of the alphabet put up around the ring as markers. A careful horse, he was afraid of brushing the letters and gave them a wide berth.

When Daniel introduced him to fences and the show ring, Winston took the same care with jumps. He naturally tucked his feet under to avoid the rails.

Daniel found it a joy to ride him at show jumping competitions because Winston seemed to want to do it all himself. He especially wanted to do it well. Winston jumped so high that even national and international riders came around to look at him. But Winston also made a loud noise in his throat whenever he ran hard, and while it was of no medical consequence, it put off buyers. He was like a new car whose engine made strange noises. It was a quirk of his, that sound — a throaty sort of rattle. He still makes it today. But when would-be buyers heard that noise in young Winston's throat, they passed him over. The years went by.

In the summer of 1983, Daniel entered Winston in four dressage competitions and took two first-place ribbons. In show jumping, he enjoyed equal success — three clear rounds in four competitions.

That same year, when Winston was seven years

old, a young Dutch rider and trainer named Bert Romp chanced by the van Hooydonk farm. Bert trains horses near the town of Tilburg, just across the border in Holland. He had come on a scouting mission, and one of the horses he noticed that day was the chestnut gelding we now know as Big Ben.

"He's no beauty," Bert told Jacobus. "He has a short neck and a big head. You can see his bones he's so skinny."

"Yes," replied Jacobus, "but if this horse falls into good hands, we will hear about him one day." While Bert debated whether to make an offer or not, Jacobus gave him some insight into the horse's character. "If a trainer uses even a little brutality on this horse," Jacobus said, "he'll get nowhere. But if a trainer gives him trust and keeps his confidence up, that trainer will get results."

No longer prince of the paddock, Winston had been saddled and trained and had shown promise in the show ring, but he remained a nervous horse. Jacobus found it hard to keep weight on him. He had that throat rattle. And so Bert was able to buy Winston for a song — 100,000 Belgian francs, or about $2,000.

Everyone was sad to see Winston go. Jacobus's wife, Louisa, had grown attached to him, and remembered with fondness how the horse would willingly lower his head to let her put his bridle on. Daniel had lost a good horse who would have taken him far in show jumping. But Jacobus stood firm. "If you are a horse breeder," he said, "then you have to sell. You can't keep them all."

Back at his own farm in Holland, Bert came to realize that the huge horse he had purchased was as timid as a mouse.

"He's scared of everything," Bert remarked to his wife. "He's afraid of water. He's afraid even of being washed." But he could jump, Bert added. "He can jump enormously high." It was the most extraordinary thing.

Bert's wife thought Winston was as tall as the clock tower in London and so she bestowed on him a new name, but still a very British one.

Big Ben.

Unfortunately for Bert, the horse proved nowhere near as reliable as that famous old clock. Bert tested him at some small competitions in Holland, where he would jump some huge fences, but not others. The aim in show jumping is to go clear: to vault the fences in order and in the time allowed. Each time horse and rider take down a fence, they are given penalty faults. It takes a special horse to do the job. The ideal jumper is quick, powerful, brave and about sixteen hands high. Much smaller than that and the fences may prove too great a hurdle. Much bigger, and the horse is usually not agile or quick enough, especially for small indoor rings.

A few Dutch and Swiss trainers came around to

look over Big Ben at Bert's farm. All pronounced him too big for the job, and too ugly to boot.

"He looks like an elephant but he handles like a thoroughbred," Bert told other riders. And like many thoroughbreds, he was easily spooked.

One day Bert walked into Big Ben's stall to change some bandages on the horse's legs. The horse seemed to be contentedly eating his hay.

"Go aside," said Bert as he bent down. "That's a good boy."

But Big Ben's temperament — spooky and aggressive at the same time — was about to hobble Bert Romp. Big Ben lashed out with a kick.

"I couldn't walk for two weeks," Bert said later. "He almost killed me, not because he was mean, but because he got scared. Big Ben was fine as long as there were no surprises."

Bert looks back on his brief time training Big Ben and he realizes there was something special about him. The horse seemed sensitive, as a thoroughbred is sensitive. But the horse also seemed to Bert, as he did to Jacobus, slow to learn.

So, when Canadian rider Ian Millar came around one day on a scouting mission of his own, Bert sold the big horse, but not for a song. Bert was starting to realize that whatever the horse's shortcomings, he had value. Bert got $45,000 for the horse — six weeks after paying $2,000 for him.

Why did Ian Millar buy him when no one else

would? Too big, some trainers said. Too ugly, they all said.

Ian had heard of this Belgian warmblood through Emile Hendrix, a Dutch trainer and rider who has sent many fine horses his way. Of all the horses Ian has bought, seventy percent have come from Emile.

Tall and solidly built, Emile has ridden for the Dutch equestrian team and knows a good horse when he sees one. If he has a tip about a horse, Ian listens. Emile knew of this horse raised in the Belgian countryside and being trained by a Dutch rider. Emile admired him.

"I don't know whether you'd like him or not," Emile told Ian. "He's a great big horse, and you've got to see him. You might really hate him, and it might be a total waste of time, but there's a chance you might find it interesting too." Ian decided it was worth a look.

Emile does have an eye for horses, Ian said to himself when he first saw the Belgian horse. There was indeed something about this one. Big Ben stood tied up in front of a stall at Bert Romp's stable, and Ian liked the belligerent way the horse looked at him. This horse had bearing. Big Ben's great height and his conformation — the particular way he is built — mean that he naturally carries his head high. Because he looks down on people, he seems arrogant.

Bert saddled him up and took him into the ring.

Time for the horse to strut his stuff for the prospective buyer.

Ian asked Bert to trot him. Ian saw that the trot appeared fine — loose and easy. The canter looked just as good. Ian was impressed by the horse's pure athleticism. On the other hand, Big Ben struck Ian as still very much a green horse. Something that all show jumpers must know is the flying change: the horse, on the move, switches from leading with one front leg to leading with the other. When Ian asked Bert to demonstrate it, Big Ben managed. But it was awkward.

When it came time for Ian to ride the horse himself, he took off Bert's saddle and put on his own. Ian got a leg up, and as soon as he settled into the saddle he knew that something was wrong. Big Ben's head went even higher, his ears lay flat against his head, and his tail whipped in circles. All signs of displeasure.

Suspecting the saddle — perhaps it pressed down on Big Ben's high withers — Ian dismounted and asked for some padding to place under the saddle. *What a sensitive horse*, he thought. This horse did not hesitate to announce that something bothered him. Ian has ridden hundreds of horses, and he figures that all but a few would have put up with that little bit of discomfort. Big Ben, as Ian would quickly learn, was not like those other horses.

When Ian got back on, the horse seemed transformed. They cantered over a small course of jumps, did some flat work, and fifteen minutes later the horse trading was done. Every bone in Ian's body told him to buy this horse. And so he did.

Big Ben would leave behind the flat fields of Belgium and Holland for the hills of southeastern Ontario. He was going to Canada. To Millar Brooke Farm.

4

Millar Brooke Farm

The first thing Big Ben did at Millar Brooke was put up a stink.

"Have all the horses been wormed?" Ian asked one of his grooms. He had bought three horses in Europe, and all needed to be vaccinated and given a routine paste-worming. The paste is squirted in the horse's mouth to destroy any worms in the horse's system.

"They're all done except for one," the groom replied, a little sheepishly.

"Which one?"

"Big Ben."

"And why not?"

"He wouldn't let us."

He wouldn't let us.

Big Ben had refused to allow anyone close enough to squirt the paste in his mouth. Worming, like blacksmiths and vets, is a fact of life for horses. But the big gelding did not see it that way.

Big Ben's strategy was to simply raise his head high — and a 17.3-hand horse can raise his head very high. The grooms were wary of his dangerous front hooves and shy of getting too close to this extremely aggressive horse. Ian countered with a strategy of his own. He put Big Ben in a section of the barn with a low ceiling where the price of raising his head was a bump. With a little help Ian got the job done, but only after a struggle.

Thus began a long and difficult period in the lives of both this young horse and his experienced rider. Training Big Ben was perhaps the greatest test of Ian Millar's legendary skills as a moulder and shaper of horses. For Big Ben had the bearing of a haughty prince and the manners of a rude peasant. He seemed not the slightest bit grateful that his new home was so splendid.

★ ★ ★

More than a hundred hectares in size, heavily wooded and bordered on the north by the Tay River, Millar

A rear view of the large barn and arena complex at Millar Brooke Farm. The veterinary hospital can be seen at left. (Photo by Jayne Huddleston)

Brooke is for show jumpers of the first rank. Here they are both pampered and challenged.

The lake country to the south of the farm is treed and rocky, a little wild. To the northwest is the historic and pretty town of Perth. Around Perth, more land is given over to pasture. It dips and rolls like a heavy sea. The pioneers who farmed here in the nineteenth century built sturdy log cabins and limestone houses, many of which still stand today. Most of the pioneer farms have since been cut up into lots, and some of the lots now have paddocks and horse barns.

Only a discreet sign on the side of the road announces Millar Brooke Farm. Hidden by trees and set back about a kilometre, the farm is secluded and private.

On the left, as you drive east along the long gravel driveway toward the farm, are six paddocks. On the right is a handsome red-brick house with black shutters and a fenced-in swimming pool. This is home to Ian and Lynn Millar, son Jonathon, and daughter Amy. The road ends at the parking area, framed by the barn, a paddock and the equine clinic run by Doctors Atack and Berthiaume.

The barn's indoor ring is amply lit by an unbroken line of windows along both sides and the east end. At each end of the ring is a complex of stables, one extending north, another south. The stables are home to thirty-two horses.

Outside is a sprawling grass course of about a dozen jumps. In the summer, it gets the full morning sun. On one side of the barn is a sand ring; on another, four more paddocks.

All in all, Millar Brooke Farm is a fancy place for horses.

★ ★ ★

Big Ben's first groom that year, 1984, was a woman named Patty Markell. She discovered the hard way that the prince does not like being disturbed while dinner (bran mash, it was) is being served. The horse had just returned from a competition out west. After spending fifty-seven hours in the horse trailer, he was in a bad mood. Patty entered the stall, hay in hand, intending to take his temperature. The thermometer, of course, does not go in the horse's mouth, but in the other end.

Ian happened by and noticed her going into the stall. He knew instinctively that it was a mistake and shouted a warning.

"No, Patty!"

She stepped back to face Ian. The next sound they heard was louder than a gunshot. It was Ben's hind hoof hitting the stall wall where Patty had been a second before.

A few months later, another groom walked into the stall with some hay and startled the sleeping Ben. In the blink of an eye, the groom was sent through the air and into the aisle. Luckily, the hay he held in front of him softened the blow and spared the groom harm. The prince, it seemed, did not like being disturbed while sleeping either.

Millar Brooke Farm aims to run smoothly, like a clock. A schedule is posted daily. Horses need to be fed, brushed, tacked up, turned out in the paddock or ridden, walked, bathed, brushed again, blanketed and fed again. The stalls are forever being mucked out and cleaned.

Time is precious at Millar Brooke; there is barely enough of it for all that needs to be done. In the barn, you can hear the sound of water splashing as horses in cross-ties are bathed, and the clomping of horses being led by grooms along the concrete walkway to and from the arena. There might be rock music playing there as Ian takes a young horse over some jumps. The blacksmith might be around, filing hooves with his rasp or putting on new shoes.

Tick-tock. Clomp-clomp. The Millar Brooke clock aims at Swiss precision.

Big Ben wanted no part of that routine. The horse struck everyone as unfriendly and troublesome. He was not just saying "No thanks," when asked to do something. "I don't wish to discuss it any further!" was more like it. The spirit, the heart, the fight — whatever it is that makes him great in the show ring — would not be reined in. Would not be controlled. Not yet anyway.

Ian likened the horse to a rebellious male

teenager in that hot zone between boyhood and manhood. Would he go to university? Or would he join a gang?

"It could go either way," Ian told his closest friends. This horse would either be great or an utter disaster.

Big Ben has hawk's eyes. He is gifted with the keenest eyesight of any horse Ian Millar has ever ridden. Those eyes are now great friends to him in the ring, but in the early days they just got him into trouble. Big Ben saw everything. And everything spooked him: a tiny squirrel poking its head around the base of a tree, even a low-flying bird. This was not a case of the lion being frightened of mice. Ian was convinced that the horse simply had a long list of evasions — excuses.

"I can't do what you're asking me to do," the horse was saying. Because. Because of the bird, the squirrel, the ditch, the water, the flags around the ring, the marching band. He was like a child in class always looking out the window, never at the teacher.

Ian was that teacher, and the first lesson was stride control. This giant horse had a canter stride that covered five-and-a-half metres. Most jumpers cover three-and-a-half to just over four metres in a canter, and officials who design courses use a series of 3.6 metre strides and half strides between jumps as the standard. Big Ben would have to shorten his naturally long stride to gather himself for the next

Big Ben enjoys the serenity of this paddock when he has the chance to relax at home. (Photo by Jayne Huddleston)

fence. If he could not master that skill, big outdoor rings would be difficult, small indoor rings impossible. He would be a bull in a china shop, just as the European trainers who passed on him said he would.

One way of teaching stride control is to place poles called cavaletti on the ground. These were invented by Italian military horsemen. By adjusting the distance between the poles, the rider can make a horse shorten or lengthen his stride. Even after Big Ben learned stride control, he still clunked his hooves on the cavaletti. He would, in time, master the highest and trickiest of jumps. But one of his quirks is that he would never figure out the cavaletti.

By 1984, Big Ben was an eight-year-old horse. Still young, but old enough that he was expected to perform. Would he go on being that troublesome teenager? Or would all his pure talent actually come to something?

If Ian had his doubts, he never displayed them. He would repeat and repeat and repeat the stride control exercises over the cavaletti. He worked on transitions. Walk to trot to canter. Canter to trot to walk. When the horse spooked, he would make him do a circle, take his mind off things. And then back to the exercise. Ian has learned the value of patience, but Big Ben was testing that patience.

By the end of the Florida circuit during the spring of 1984 — his first real taste of competition — Big Ben was a little farther ahead. Not much, though.

Other riders looked at the huge gelding and did the kind thing. They said nothing. For riders at this level, a new horse is like a new car or a new coat. The rule of etiquette is that others are supposed to notice and say something nice. No one said a thing about Big Ben. The only comment came from an American rider.

"He sure is big."

★ ★ ★

Back at Millar Brooke Farm, Big Ben was still an unruly pupil. Until the day, that summer of '84, that a substitute teacher handled class. It marked a turning point.

Eve Mainwaring had been there at Bert Romp's farm in Holland the day Ian bought the horse. Born in Estonia but of German descent, the tall, freckled woman is a fine rider and trainer who befriended Ian Millar a long time ago and has learned to trust his instincts. She had agreed then and there to be his partner — to pay for half the purchase price of Ben.

Afterwards, Eve occasionally drove over from her own horse farm in Brockville, Ontario to see how the young prospect was doing and to ride him. One day that summer, the horse spooked in the indoor ring with Eve on board. No surprise there. The surprise for Ian, who was watching, came when Eve gave him a smart slap with the crop for his misbehaviour.

Oh-oh, thought Ian. *The big guy is going to explode.* But Ben did not explode.

Ian Millar rides Big Ben in one of their early competitions. (Photo by Jayne Huddleston)

A few minutes later, he spooked again. Again Eve used the stick. Still no outburst from the horse. During the rest of the ride, he stuck to the business at hand. He was learning to take direction without objecting.

Back in the stall, too, his unyielding character appeared to soften. Big Ben had never much liked people. He never sought affection, unlike those school horses who stop in the centre of the ring so the instructor can give them a reassuring pat. He never nosed around for a carrot, or nickered at the approach of his groom. But he was warming up a little.

A few weeks after Eve Mainwaring introduced Big Ben to the crop, Ian took the horse to a small summer competition in Montreal. New tournament. New course. Here were circumstances that would have rattled Big Ben the previous spring. But he jumped everything easily in Montreal. His focus remained sharp.

Rugged and proud-looking, he carried his head high in the ring. People who saw him jump once did not soon forget him. Here was a great big horse, yet one who moved like a cat. He possessed amazing balance. Had all this power. All this effortless grace.

A week later, Ian took him to a show in Edmonton and moved him up into ever-higher classes. Nothing fazed him. On Sunday, Ian jumped him in the grand prix. French for "big prize," grand prix competitions force horse and rider to excel. This was the biggest test of Big Ben's young career. He came in second.

Rarely do horses leap into the elite grand prix world so quickly. The bigger fences, the tougher courses defeat them in the beginning. Riders usually move a new jumper up cautiously, and will often move a horse down again if he shows any sign of losing confidence. Big Ben vaulted almost overnight into the big leagues of show jumping. He had been in Canada less than a year and despite a shaky start, he had quite suddenly become a grand prix jumper.

Ian Millar with Big Ben (left) and former stablemate Warrior. (Perth Courier photo)

5

Lord of the Ring

In 1984, Big Ben was still inexperienced but beginning to show promise. It was an Olympic year, and Ian Millar had been chosen to ride for the Canadian equestrian team in Los Angeles, California. He wrestled with the notion of taking Big Ben to these Olympics.

The fences in Olympic competition are a great deal higher than they are even in grand prix classes. Sometimes, these high fences and tricky courses can destroy a horse's confidence. A horse can leave the

Games dispirited, defeated. That horse may never be the same again. Going to the Olympic Games, then, is a huge step for a young horse.

Ian's top horse at the time was a gelding named Warrior, a proven grand prix horse. Prior to the '84 Games Warrior had pulled a muscle in his back, but he was close to recovery. Big Ben had done well at the Olympic trials, yet was still young to face such a stiff test. Hedging his bets, Ian took both Warrior and Big Ben to Los Angeles and at the last minute opted for Big Ben.

A gold medal in the individual event in Los Angeles would have been nothing short of a miracle for Ian and his young horse. No miracle occurred. But in the team event, Big Ben and Ian did better than any other Canadian combination. They helped Canada to a respectable fourth-place finish.

Back in Belgium, Jacobus van Hooydonk was watching television coverage of Olympic show jumping. Into the ring came a Canadian rider on a horse called Big Ben. Jacobus almost fell off his chair. He would have known that horse anywhere. That was Winston! Nine months after being sold for a pittance, he was an Olympic competitor. Jacobus felt a stirring of pride, tinged with regret that he had let Winston go — and for so little. Jacobus sighed and went back to his television to watch more horses going over more fences.

By 1986, Big Ben's star was rising. The tight little

Big Ben jumping in his first Olympic Games, in Los Angeles, 1984. (Photo by Jayne Huddleston)

world of show jumping had begun to notice this huge horse. A string of grand prix victories on Big Ben that year helped Ian become the top-ranked rider in North America. No Canadian rider had ever achieved this standing. At the World Cup in Gothenburg, Sweden, in 1986, audiences got a hint of what was to come: Big Ben came second in this demanding three-part competition.

The Pan American Games of 1987 were held in the flat country outside Indianapolis, Indiana. The sprawling grounds had been created on the site of an old county fair. Rustic stands had been fashioned out of barn board. The summer in Indiana that year was hot, the kind of weather for frying eggs on sidewalks.

Big Ben had been jumping superbly before the Games. But just prior to the first round of the team competition, Ian noticed something — a slight stutter — in the way Ben moved his right hind leg. Sandi Patterson, by now his groom, led him forward a little more, and then the soreness was as plain as day. Round one loomed a mere fifteen minutes away.

Five precious minutes were lost in finding the blacksmith. He removed the shoe from the horse's right hind hoof and used what is called a hoof-tester to apply pressure. When one spot was tested, Big Ben pulled back his hoof. This confirmed what they suspected. The source of Big Ben's discomfort was infection in that hoof.

Ian had only a few minutes to think, and his thinking went like this: *This is a professional athlete and a pampered one. If he jumps now, we risk no long-term damage. The vet has given the go-ahead. Big Ben may be uncomfortable and he may jump badly. But let us try.*

In the ring, the horse compensated. He landed more on the toe of that sore foot and placed fifth. But afterwards, he clearly felt delicate and he kept his weight off the painful foot.

Back in the barn, Sandi soaked the foot in a tub of hot water and Epsom salts. Big Ben would tolerate this for forty-five seconds, and then pull it out. Later it was Ian's turn to play keep-the-foot-in-the-tub with Big Ben. And so it went all night long. They also walked him on asphalt with something called an Easy Boot, a plastic overshoe designed to stimulate the infection and draw it out. Finally, they tried a bran poultice. No luck.

Next morning, the blacksmith attempted to put Ben's shoe back on for the competition. The horse would have none of it. Blacksmiths are not his favourite people anyway, and there was no way he was going to let this burly man or any of his pals put that shoe on his sore foot. He would not lift it.

Smart about horses, Lynn Millar remembers the moment well. "He's never been a horse you could order around in the stall," she says. "He'll just stand there and look at you. But if you ask him nicely, he'll respond. Ben will do anything for Sandi. It's a matter of trust."

With time running out, Sandi led the unhappy horse to his stall. Ian knew that things can often be accomplished in a stall — the horse's home, after all — that cannot be done elsewhere. Ian's daughter Amy, then ten years old, held a fan so the breeze cooled Ben this hot, hot day. She also fed him carrots. Then Sandi performed one of those little miracles that sometimes happen between horses and humans. She ran her hand down his right hind leg and simply said, "Lift your leg, Bennie." The great gelding may have sighed inwardly, but he did as he was told. The blacksmith seized the opportunity and got the shoe on in less than a minute.

Ian and Big Ben went into the ring and pulled off a clear round. On the way out, Lynn noticed that the abscess had popped out at the coronet band — where the hoof meets the hair of the skin. The infection was now out of the hoof. Now perfectly sound, the horse went on to jump yet another clean round while helping the Canadian team to a gold medal. The icing on the cake came when Ian and Big Ben won a second gold medal at these Pan American Games, this one in the individual competition.

The moral of the story: never count this horse out.

Later that year, in September, Ian and Big Ben were in Calgary for a week of show jumping that

Ian Millar accepts one of the two gold medals he and Big Ben won at the 1987 Pan American Games. (Canadian Sport Images)

would culminate with the Spruce Meadows Masters. This is an Olympic-scale grand prix that always attracts Olympic riders because the prizes are tops in the world. When Ian rode Big Ben into the international ring at Spruce Meadows that cool clear Sunday and tipped his hat before starting the course, he and his horse had already established themselves as favourites.

Still, the chances of winning are always slim when the best compete for that trophy. When the last rider was done and it became clear that Ian and Big Ben had won, the audience gave them a standing ovation. They stood while the prizes were handed out, and began cheering again as Ian rode Ben in the victory gallop. They were still cheering long after the last horse and rider had left the ring.

In 1988, the top forty-five riders in the world competed in the World Cup in Gothenburg, Sweden. Big Ben had come so far so quickly that the experts were predicting an easy victory. Ian had been ranked top rider in the world, and Big Ben had achieved star status.

But the obstacles this week were not just in the ring. Although he won the first stage — a test of agility and quickness — on Thursday, it was clear by the second round on Friday that Big Ben had contracted a virus. He ran a temperature and even showed signs, for the first time in his life, of colic. Still, he took down only one rail and managed a fourth-place finish.

Going into the final round, Ian and Ben were leading.

By Saturday — a rest day during the competition — Ian had Sandi walk the horse, but nothing more strenuous than that. In the final two rounds on Sunday, he took down only one rail the first time out and went clear in the second round. The horse had to dig deep into his great well of strength to jump those last fences because the virus had sapped him. Yet he won.

Every great show jumper in the world was there, and Big Ben had beaten them all.

Then came the 1988 Olympic Games at Seoul, Korea. Everyone had high hopes for Big Ben and Ian Millar — they were expected to bring home the gold. During the Games, Ian wore a green arm band with his competition number — 126. It was not a lucky number.

Fifteenth place is not where you expect to find Big Ben. Ian wondered later whether the virus lingered and played a part in the horse's poor performance at the Olympics. Maybe the unusually ornate jumps — based on themes from Korean mythology — threw him off. Whatever it was, the 1988 Games were a washout for Ben. Some experts concluded that the horse had lost his edge. But Ian had no doubt that the mighty Ben would come back. And, of course, he did. Roaring back.

To follow the history of the Ian/Ben combination is to ride a roller coaster. A brilliant victory here, then

Big Ben going over an elaborate jump at the 1988 Seoul Olympics, where high hopes for a medal were dashed. (Photo by Jayne Huddleston)

a crushing defeat there, followed by brilliant victory again. In show jumping, what goes up must surely come down. And Big Ben and his fans have certainly had their ups and downs. Unfortunately, some of the downs have taken place at the worst of times — Olympic Games.

It's too bad that Big Ben cannot say how he feels about winning and losing. He has certainly had his share of both. On examination, his record reveals a pattern. Just when many think he has lost it, gotten too old or had one operation too many, he comes back better than ever. This horse has heart.

Witness the events of 1989. *Horses* magazine devoted an entire issue to the 1989 World Cup in Tampa, Florida. A colour photograph introduced the series of articles, and it showed Mr. Millar and Mr. Ben leaping a fence under a banner reading "Winners and Champions." The caption read: "The World's Best Rider was in total command, and the mighty Big Ben was at his all-time peak. They made it look easy, winning all three phases of the competition . . . prevailing against the best in the world, Ian and his extraordinary horse set a new standard of achievement in the sport of showjumping."

There were forty-seven horses from all over the world in the field. In the first phase, Ben went clear and was almost three seconds faster than the second-place horse. Phase two featured two jumpoffs — races against the clock. Ben's appearance in the ring was greeted by huge applause. In the first jumpoff, he rattled the back rail of the first fence . . . but it stayed up. Once again, he went clear. Only five horses of the forty-seven did that. In the second jumpoff, Ben took down fence number six — his first fault of the competition — but his time was exceptionally fast.

In the final phase of the competition, two more gruelling rounds, Ben tapped the second fence but it stayed up and once more he went clear. The applause, both before and after the round, was deafening. The crowd sensed the historic nature of what was happening. In the final round, Ian and Ben again went clear with nary a rub. The crowd was on its feet now. They whooped. They hollered. They cheered.

Ben and Ian had done what no other horse and rider combination had ever done. They had won all three phases of the World Cup, *and* they had won back-to-back World Cups. John Quirk, *Horses* editor and an equestrian journalist who has covered the sport all over North America and Europe, called it "an accomplishment for the ages."

Ian later said that he felt like a passenger on Big Ben's back. "All I did," he said, "was escort this horse around the courses. The hero here is Big Ben."

6

A
Day In
the Life

Since 1987, Sandi Patterson has been an integral part of Big Ben's life. During all the road trips, the almost daily tacking up and conditioning, the competitions all over the world, she has been the one constant. At big tournaments, she never leaves him. She even sleeps on a cot outside his stall as a security measure.

Ian worries that large crowds might begin to unnerve Big Ben. Perhaps someone might carelessly, or even purposely, feed the horse something that would hurt him, or show up in random drug testing and cost the horse and rider a victory. Sandi is Big Ben's guardian.

Before coming to Millar Brooke, Sandi operated a small business training ponies and teaching children to ride. When she wanted instruction for herself, she sought it from Ian Millar. This is like going to Wayne Gretzky for hockey lessons. Ian Millar is a perfectionist. Every day he issues a challenge — to his horses, grooms, vet and blacksmith. "Do better," he says to them and to himself.

It makes him a tough teacher. Whatever illusions Sandi may have had about her own riding ability, they were soon dashed.

But she stayed on. Ian needed a groom for the annual Florida circuit in 1987, and that sounded fine to Sandi. She signed on for that trip, and never left. She eventually became barn manager at Millar Brooke, where she educates other grooms about the great expectations at Ian Millar's farm.

Ian is an engaging, energetic man with a wonderful sense of humour. But he is also a champion and he will not tolerate sloppy work from anyone.

"What's it like working for a perfectionist?" a journalist once asked Sandi.

"Maybe he's not the *only* perfectionist at Millar Brooke," Sandi replied.

Sandi still rides. She rides the horse many people would give anything to ride. She exercises Big Ben

The front view of the tidy barn and arena complex at Millar Brooke Farm. The second floor contains offices and apartments for grooms. (Photo by Jayne Huddleston)

out in the arena, a jockey of a woman on a giant of a horse.

Though the road trips are never-ending and the hours of work exhausting, the rewards are many. Sandi feels a part of something special, and the five to seven hours a day she devotes to Big Ben are an undeniable part of his success.

★ ★ ★

Big Ben's day begins at 7:00 A.M., when Sandi comes around and puts fresh water in his bucket. Then he gets his hydroponically grown barley grass, harvested from a neon-lit refrigerator that occupies a large cupboard at one end of the indoor ring.

Sandi irreverently calls it "the grass machine" and it works like this: barley seed and water are placed in a thirty by sixty centimetre plastic tray on the bottom rack of the glassed-in refrigerator. As the seeds sprout and grow, the tray is moved onto the rack above, and then the one after that. In a week, the tray has reached the top rack. By then it contains a sheaf that looks like the end of a square broom. The new grass is a bright lime green in colour. Rich in bacteria and moisture, it is supposed to be an easily digestible food. Ever since Big Ben's second attack of colic in 1991, barley grass has been a regular part of his diet.

The University of Guelph had been testing the grass on some of its patients while Big Ben was there for his second colic surgery. "You'll think I'm crazy,"

Big Ben frolics at home in his paddock. (Photo by Jayne Huddleston)

Sandi said to Ian one day, "but I want to buy a grass machine." And so they did.

At 7:15 A.M., breakfast continues at Millar Brooke. Sandi gives Big Ben one or two flakes of hay.

At 7:30, he gets his grains — one scoop of bran, one scoop of what Purina calls the "Ben" mix (a roughage food combining pellets, oats and molasses), and some Metamucil — all meant to keep his digestive system moving along as it should. Once a day he gets mineral oil, yet another way of keeping Big Ben's troublesome bowels loose.

While he is eating, Sandi mucks out his stall. Unlike some, Sandi notes with a little pride, Big Ben is a neat horse.

At 8:30, in the summer anyway, he is turned out in his paddock for an hour. He prefers the company of Future Vision in the paddock next door, and what Big Ben wants, Big Ben usually gets. Sandi may pass the hour leaning on the fence, watching him and keeping him company.

Even on bitter days in January, Big Ben and the other horses may visit their snowy paddocks. Ian Millar knows a thing or two about horses, and he thinks that the horses need to be outside every day, even in winter — unless the paddocks are icy.

"It's good," he says, "to put them out there with their turn-out rugs and just let them be horses."

After the paddock visit, about 9:30, Sandi takes Big Ben back to his stall where he drinks water and relaxes. She grooms him and curry-brushes him. Perhaps she vacuums the loose hairs from his back. For the next half hour, he is fitted with the electromagnetic machine, a spider's web of wires and tiny suction cups. The treatment relaxes him and increases circulation to the muscles across the back. If a competition is around the corner, Sandi will also use the laser machine, a battery-operated device that targets acupuncture points on the body. This, too, helps to relax Big Ben's muscles.

By now it is time to tack him up in preparation for his daily ride by Ian. For such a big strong horse, the tack is mild. The bit is a plain egg butt snaffle, with a running martingale. Most horses are fitted with a heavier bit, most big horses a heavier one still. "If you see a horse in the ring with a heavy metal bit," says Sandi, "there's some communication missing between that horse and that rider."

Big Ben's breast plate is elastic, chosen because it allows him more freedom at the shoulder. Very superstitious, Sandi uses the same pair of tendon boots that Ben has always worn — old-style, felt-lined ones. They are not even made any more, so Sandi keeps doctoring the old ones, which have more padding than the newer models. Ben has a habit of catching himself on the ankle. These old tendon boots protect him.

Ian usually rides him by 10:00 A.M. If, for some reason, that does not happen, Ben begins to show his displeasure. He bobs his head up and down and paws the ground, digging holes in his stall. He thinks he should be ridden first. For a groom to lead another horse past his stall, a tacked-up, ready-to-ride horse, is like waving a red flag before a bull.

"He's a horse with a lot of character," concludes Sandi. "He thinks we are here to take care of him. He expects all the extras. When he wants to go out, he wants to be first out and first ridden. If he's not ridden by 10 o'clock he gets mad. He'll buck and twirl when it comes time to ride him. His electromagnetic machine has a buzzer that sounds when the time is up. When that buzzer goes, he wants off. Right away. He starts bobbing his head and pawing the ground."

If Ian is not on the farm, someone else may ride him. Ben sizes the rider up immediately and may appear unresponsive or just plain dumb. The rider may be intimidated and the horse knows it. The rider has a crop but hesitates to use it. "I'm Big Ben," the horse is saying. "You gonna hit *me* with that thing?"

Sandi will sometimes turn him loose in the ring, and if he is excited he will charge up to her and rear at the last second. Or he may buck. He may circle her as if kept on an invisible lunge line, and keep doing it until she tells him to go away. A vocal horse, he will call to her, nickering like a colt to its mother. Out of the show ring, he is a playful giant.

It is a joy to watch a gifted rider such as Ian ride any horse. But when he rides Big Ben — even at Millar

Brooke's outdoor ring for forty-five minutes of conditioning — something happens. It is a little like watching a painter working up a tiny sketch, a preamble, perhaps, to a masterpiece. As you watch, you are drawn in. The more intently you watch, the more there is to see and the more you imagine yourself out there on that great big horse.

One warm sunny morning in June of 1993, I sat under an apple tree and watched them. One of the farm's two cats, Ginger, sidled up alongside. Then others joined in: Sandi's Jack Russell terrier, Brie, Amy's two Corgis, Amis and Andy, Lynn's aged spaniel, Sandy, and Jonathon's golden Labrador, J.J. We formed a makeshift audience. Out in the ring, Ian was wearing a red golf shirt, a white baseball cap, and soft leather chaps over his jeans. The chaps made Ian look a little bowlegged, like a ranch hand. He was taking Ben around the perimeter of the course, clockwise, effortlessly shifting gears on the horse.

The tiny audience saw that loose, easy trot of Ben's, the one that Ian liked so much when he first saw it in Holland. Then Ian slowed the trot right down. The two looked as if they were barely moving forward. It seemed certain that at the very next step the trot would simply fold into a walk. Puffs of dust were being kicked up by Ben's hind hoofs, but the white socks were still clearly visible from behind. How could this big horse and his lanky rider sustain that slow-motion trot? Inevitably, like a plane throttled down, the trot would surely stall.

It did not stall. The control never faltered. A few minutes later, Ian nudged Big Ben into a faster trot, then a canter. They formed figure eights as they took this jump and then that one. Such finesse in one so big, we thought. Ben was not holding his head high, as he does during actual competition. He was coasting over these small jumps, exerting himself as little as possible. Like many great athletes, he cannot get up for practices the way he can for the big game.

But even in the schooling ring there was much to admire: the neat folding of the legs as Ben vaulted. The little thunder of his hooves that stopped with every leap and picked up again when he landed. The way Ian sat him, rooted in the saddle, hands quiet. Two partners were out there communicating with each other, but it was all invisible and silent. A lot was understood without ever being said.

At one point, Ben shied at something. Ian halted him. Started him up again. The elegant stride was immediately regained.

The ginger cat climbed up the apple tree for a better view. The dogs, they had seen it all before. They moved elsewhere for another round of wrestling.

When Ian had finished working Big Ben, Sandi walked him off and then led him back to his stall. He would get more food there. The meals come four times a day at Millar Brooke. In the afternoon, Big Ben will typically go out to his paddock again.

The inside of the main barn at Millar Brooke Farm. Ben's stall is on the right, by the wooden door. (Photo by Jayne Huddleston)

But Ben will stay out in the paddock for no more than an hour. It makes sense, perhaps, that a horse named after a clock has an uncanny sense of time. Anything more than an hour and Big Ben starts to nicker at Sandi. He wants his stall.

Sandi will often lie down next to him while he grazes the grass. At these times, she leans on her elbows and crosses her legs so that one foot is in the air. Ever playful, Ben cannot resist. He will remove that dangled shoe if it is loose on her foot and toss it in the air. He will do the same with the crop.

Big Ben likes to chew on things: his nose band, his bridle, a crop. Once he was chewing on Ian's crop and he managed to remove the heavy leather handle — a modified golf club grip.

"I was afraid he was going to swallow the handle," says Sandi, laughing now as she did not then. "I had my hand in his mouth up to my wrist. He finally spat it out. Like a cigar."

Two things he cannot abide are trains and plastic bags. If he hears the sound of a train at a tournament, he will begin to walk nervously, and he will keep walking until the train has gone. Plastic holds equal terror for him. Draw a carrot from a plastic bag and he will shy. Witnesses to such an event are astonished that such a big animal can dart sideways and backwards so suddenly.

When Ian was training him that first year in Florida, he recalls, "Garbage pails just about killed

Ian Millar and Big Ben jumping the plank at Spruce Meadows. (Photo by Shawn Hamilton/Clix)

The mighty Ben after yet another victory. (Photo by Shawn Hamilton/Clix)

At the 1988 Olympic Games. This is where Big Ben's problems began: the pagoda was the first of three jumps to fall, eliminating him from the competition. (Photo by Jayne Huddleston)

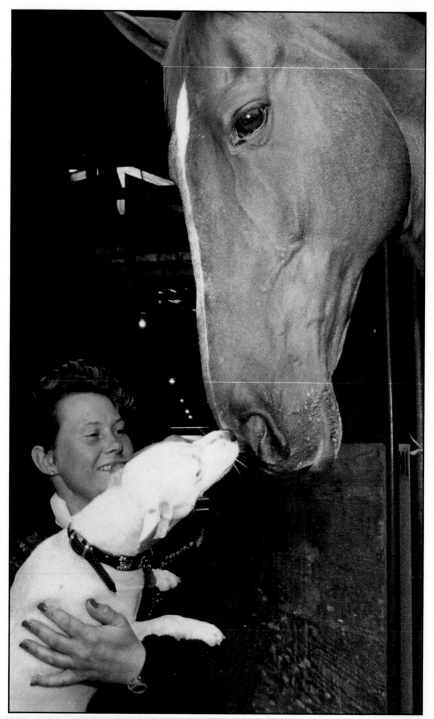

Ben greets Sandi Patterson's Jack Russell terrier, Brie. The dog, too, is devoted to this horse. (Calgary Herald photo)

The 1991 Nations' Cup at Spruce Meadows: Big Ben's reactions are so quick and he knows his job so well that when he realized in mid-air that this was a spread jump, not an upright, he still recovered and managed a clean round. (Photo by Jayne Huddleston)

Ian Millar and Big Ben celebrate their grand prix win in 1991 at the Spruce Meadows Masters in Calgary. (Photo by Shawn Hamilton/Clix)

Big Ben plays with his brush. (Photo by Suzanne Smith)

Big Ben relaxes in his paddock at Millar Brooke Farm. (Photo by Jayne Huddleston)

Look at the intensity on Ian Millar's face as he guides Big Ben over a fence. Inset: the crowd looks on tensely. (Photo by Jayne Huddleston; inset, Prime Time Sports Photography Ltd.)

In the training ring at Spruce Meadows. (Photo by Shawn Hamilton/Clix)

The bonnet on Big Ben's head is meant to keep distracting insects out of his ears. (Photo by Jayne Huddleston)

Big Ben and Sandi Patterson in Calgary, just after both survived the terrible highway accident in 1992. (Calgary Herald photo)

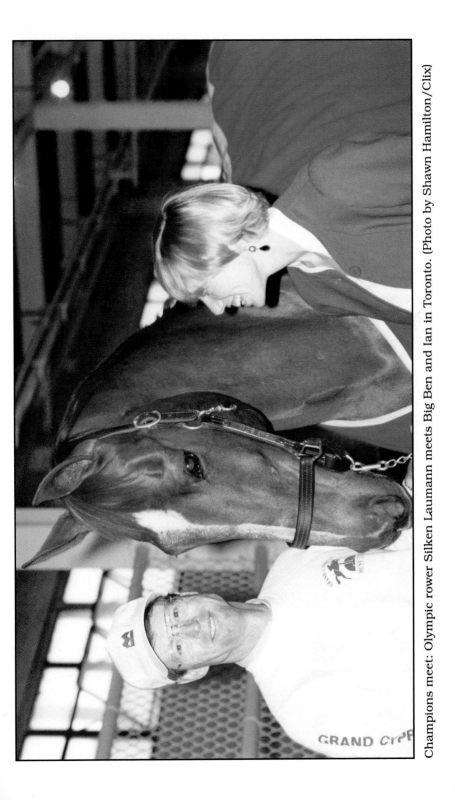

Champions meet: Olympic rower Silken Laumann meets Big Ben and Ian in Toronto. (Photo by Shawn Hamilton/Clix)

Big Ben's record at Spruce Meadows in Calgary may never be duplicated. He has won the Masters grand prix twice and the gruelling derby six times. (Photo by Jayne Huddleston)

Ian and Big Ben during a victory gallop at Spruce Meadows. Inset: yet another trophy. (Photo by Shawn Hamilton/Clix; inset, Prime Time Sports Photography Ltd.)

Big Ben and a young fan at the Royal Winter Fair in Toronto, 1993.
(Photo by Paul Heersink)

me. A plastic bag rippling in the wind would drive him crazy. Even today, when those bags start to blow and you're on Ben, you better buckle up." Ben will buck and twirl and he has, on a couple of occasions, sent Ian crashing to the ground. He has also spun with Sandi aboard, but never more than she can handle. The horse seems to know exactly how much Sandi can tolerate.

Lonesome Dove, a stablemate of Big Ben's, is clearly his love interest. He absolutely adores her. They nicker to each other often and are paired in the van for long trips. Ever since they both competed at Stuttgart, Germany in 1989, says Sandi, they have been fast friends.

"She's his girlfriend," Sandi confides. "If she ever dumped him he would be really upset."

Once a week is bath day. Ben lays down certain conditions before he allows this to happen. If Sandi puts him in the cross-ties, he refuses to lower his head to let it be washed. However, if Sandi *removes* the cross-ties, down comes the head. This is Big Ben's version of "Let's Make A Deal."

At Millar Brooke, Sandi's apartment is located directly above Big Ben's stall. Because he is so vocal, and because Sandi listens from her room as he routinely moves about, she knows his habits. At 11 o'clock he goes to the bathroom. At midnight he lies down. At 2:00 A.M. he rises briefly. At 5:00 A.M. he is still quiet and Sandi may check on him if he is not.

Then it is up for breakfast at 7:00 A.M.

At some point during most days, Sandi will tack up Big Ben. She goes into the lounge past Big Ben's stall. There saddles are neatly arrayed on wooden trees, each bridle and halter on a wooden hook, the name of the horse they belong to etched underneath on brass plates. Occupying every corner and wall are red ribbons, silver trophies, victory blankets. Many of those belong to Big Ben.

She has tacked him up thousands of times, and anyone who sees the process for the first time might be amused at the sight of one so small attending to one so big. But anyone who has witnessed the ritual of Sandi tacking up Ben is seeing proof of a great friendship between a horse and a human.

If he chose not to be tacked up, he need only raise his head. Sandi would require either a long ladder or a good set of wings. Ben lowers his head when she asks him to, and, like most horses, closes his eyes as the tack passes over them. He knows that she is the most loyal friend he has in this world. He nickers to her when she passes his stall. He comes to her when she calls him. She lets him scratch his nose on her back and talks to him constantly whenever she is around him. They are pals.

"I love him," says Sandi, and she means it.

They say absence makes the heart grow fonder. But when Sandi leaves Millar Brooke for a few days, Ben takes it hard. He nips at the grooms attending

The bond between Sandi and Big Ben is very special. On the rare occasions that she leaves Millar Brooke Farm, he pouts for days. (Photo by Jayne Huddleston)

him, not to harm them, but perhaps to show his displeasure. The only time he nickers at Lynn Millar is when Sandi is away. In Sandi's absence, Lynn will have to do. And when Sandi returns, the groom gets the big cold shoulder. Ben pouts.

He will stand in his stall with his back to her and refuse to come to her. No nicker. Not a hint of recognition. He will keep up this sulking for days. No other horse at Millar Brooke Farm does this. Finally, he finds it in that great heart of his to forgive her, and they are pals again.

Until the next time she leaves.

7

On the Road

"Good evening, ladies and gentleman, this is your captain speaking. Welcome to Lufthansa flight 147. We'll be leaving Montreal shortly en route to Frankfurt, Germany. I would like to welcome you all aboard, and a special welcome to some horses we have travelling in the rear cabin, including the great Canadian show jumper, Big Ben. . . ."

Big Ben has seen the world. He has been all over North America, of course, in horse vans. And he has travelled widely in Europe and parts of Asia for World

Big Ben on the tarmac at Calgary airport. (Photo by Todd Korol)

Cups and Olympic Games and grand prix.

He is not the best traveller. Those close to him, such as Sandi, can sense his joy when the horse van swings down the lane of Millar Brooke Farm after a long journey and his paddock comes into view.

The stress of plane travel takes a lot out of Big Ben. He can lose up to sixty-five kilos — almost ten percent of his total weight — in one trip. To keep him healthy on the road, Lynn Millar puts her faith in a herbal concoction for horses available only in Germany. She calls them "magic drops" and twenty are put into Big Ben's food before each long trip to boost his immune system. It seems to help.

On a typical trip to Europe, Big Ben and Sandi travel by horse trailer to the airport. There is no standing in line at check-in counters for Ben. The horse van drives directly into the huge cargo buildings, where the horses are loaded into specially designed stalls that resemble a two-horse trailer. The stalls are then linked, like the coaches of a train, and hauled onto the tarmac.

There a hydraulically operated lift, called a "high loader," raises several stalls at a time until they sit level with the plane's cargo loading door. Rollers on both the loader and inside the plane then move horses and stalls to a designated spot. The whole mechanized operation takes only a few minutes.

The horse has no real notion of being inside a plane or, later, of being airborne. This is a good thing.

The plane is typically a Boeing 747 Combi: it may look like any other 747 on the outside, but only the front of the plane is for passengers. The rear section is for animals and other special cargo. You may, then, have flown in the company of horses — or even Big Ben himself — and never realized it. Not all pilots announce the fact that animals are on board.

A specially trained flight attendant monitors the loading and unloading and makes frequent trips back to the horses to ensure that all is well. As with some human travellers, the most stressful part of air travel for horses is takeoff and landing. On takeoff, the plane vibrates and climbs steeply, making it hard for horses to keep their balance; on landing, the tires screech and the plane may brake quickly, again upsetting the horses' balance. These moments can inspire panic among four-legged passengers. Takeoff and landing can also play havoc with air pressure, and just as humans are sometimes given candies to suck on because the act of swallowing helps ease the pressure on the ears, horses are given carrots to munch.

The attendant hopes that it is never needed, but on board is a bag containing a drug to put a horse down in case of emergency. If a horse ever broke loose, he could put his foot through the wall of a plane. The sudden loss of pressure could endanger the aircraft and everyone on it. Only a small number of horses have to be tranquillized for plane travel —

three to four percent — and Big Ben is not among them.

As the pilot said, Big Ben did travel to Germany — in October of 1989. Show jumping is a major sport in Europe, as popular there as hockey is in Canada. When Big Ben goes to Europe, he is a star, and even his groom is asked to sign autographs. In Stuttgart that year, expectations of victory were great. Anything less than a top ribbon and Europeans would wonder what had happened to the mighty Ben.

With Sandi on the same plane, Big Ben travelled in the company of Lonesome Dove. The horses would arrive in Stuttgart several days ahead of Ian, giving them time to adjust to their new surroundings.

At Frankfurt, Germany, the plane landed. The horses were to be unloaded here and put in twenty-four-hour quarantine. This is normal procedure when horses cross borders. The intention is to reduce the likelihood of horses infecting one another with diseases. From Frankfurt, the horses would travel by road to Stuttgart.

It was a Saturday evening, and most workers in the big cargo building had gone to supper. One lone man was there to help Sandi take the horses out, and Sandi needed him to hold Big Ben while she moved Lonesome Dove to another stall. The man took one look at the giant horse and declined. So Sandi moved "Dovie," as she calls her, out first. Ben must have thought he was being abandoned. While Sandi was out of sight trying to find the right stall, she could hear Big Ben screaming for Lonesome Dove. More disturbingly, Sandi could hear the sound of hoof on wood as the big gelding struggled to get out of his one-and-a-half-metre stall.

Sandi can move pretty quickly when she has to. She left Lonesome Dove tied in one corner of the building, amid the crates of cats and dogs. When she got back, there was Ben with one leg up over the stall. She managed to back him up so he could get the leg off.

Eventually, Big Ben and Lonesome Dove got to Stuttgart without further incident. Ben had a big bruise on his chest from the mishap at the airport, but otherwise he seemed fine.

When he got to his stall under a huge white tent at the Stuttgart grounds, more than a dozen television, radio and print reporters and photographers were waiting. They wanted shots of Ian and his horse, shots of Ian exercising him, and answers to their questions. Ian's photograph and a story about him and Big Ben made the daily newspaper *Stuttgart Zeitung* and several other newspapers.

Though it was late October in southern Germany, the days were warm and sunny. By the time the jet-lagged Ian rode Big Ben his first morning in Stuttgart, a Tuesday, it had been three days between rides. Ian looked unhappy as he tried to get the horse down to business. Big Ben seemed more intent on goofing off.

The Stuttgart show is for older, experienced horses. Even getting from the stables to the competition area is an adventure. Grooms have to lead their horses across a busy four-lane avenue. Police stop traffic to let the horses cross, but even grand prix veterans can get spooky at the crossing. Younger horses would be even more inclined to panic.

On Thursday, Big Ben somehow *knew* he was going to compete that day. His routine that morning was the same as it had been for the past two days. Yet he knew. All day he pawed the ground and bobbed his head in agitation.

The competition took place in the indoor ring, called the Martin-Schleyer-Halle. It is also used as a velodrome, and if you look underneath the bleachers you can see the banked wooden track where the cyclists do their sprinting. The Halle had been lavishly decorated with fresh flowers from Holland, as befits a tournament more polished than the bugles in a brass band. The tournament runs precisely on time. The courses are tough. The horses and riders are the best in Europe.

This was Big Ben's first indoor competition of the year, and he sometimes takes a while to adjust. Sure enough, the Thursday start went badly. Ian and Big Ben took down two jumps: the top plank of one and the first vertical in a triple combination.

On Friday night, there were signs that Big Ben was rounding into form. He had the fastest time of any horse in the competition, and made one brilliant inside turn that left the crowd gasping. However, he also took down one rail. Unless he came up big in the grand prix on Sunday, Ian would return to Millar Brooke Farm empty-handed.

Sunday morning, Big Ben seemed truly agitated. He wanted to go. And he got his chance early, for Ian drew sixth position in a flashy field of forty-one horse-and-rider combinations. All the great British riders — including John Whitaker and his fabulous grey horse Milton — were here, along with the powerful German, Austrian, Swiss and French riders.

At first, the course seemed easy. Three of five horses went clear. Big Ben and Ian did the same, and while their time was well within the time allowed, it was slow. After that, the clear rounds came harder. Especially tricky were two jumps early in the course — narrow verticals with a long gallop the length of the ring between them. Some horses made the first one, but the long gallop excited them and their riders failed to collect their mounts before the second. Other horses knocked down both verticals. By the end of the first round, twenty-six of the best in the world had been eliminated. Only fifteen combinations would go on to round two.

Once again, Big Ben went clear, and his time was quick. Astonishingly quick. Ben is an old hand at all

Big Ben and Ian Millar pull off a dramatic win in the grand prix of Stuttgart. (Photo by Jayne Huddleston)

this, but the usual format at grand prix competitions is one round followed by a jumpoff — a race against the clock over a shortened course. And because Ben was convinced that he was in the jumpoff, not round two, he went fast. Ian struggled to hold him back. They managed to keep all the rails up, including the one remaining narrow vertical — this time approached from the other end of the ring. No other horse came close to matching his time.

Five horses went clear in round two and earned the right to proceed to the jumpoff. The crowd was very animated by this time, shouting out special encouragement to the German rider, Kurt Maier, Jr., on Leon. The other riders were all world-class equestrians: Jos Lansink of the Netherlands, Thomas Frühmann of Austria, Nick Skelton of Great Britain, and the Canadian, Ian Millar on Big Ben. A prize of 30,000 Deutschmarks (about $20,000) would go to the winner.

Big Ben was up first. The time allowed was forty-seven seconds, and as he lofted over the jumps, cutting corners and galloping across the ring, he seemed not to be racing at all. A horse in a hurry can come undone, but not this one. He maintained his distinctively long stride; the head and tail stayed high. Ben is what horse people call "a big mover": he eats up the distance without seeming to rush.

Up in the stands, amid all the seated German supporters, a lone Canadian fan had risen to his feet.

As Big Ben successfully leapt every fence, the man pumped his clenched right fist and muttered "Yes-yes-yes!" Each time he spoke a little louder, and by the last fence, he was talking to himself. "Come on Ben, come on." Some of the crowd turned to face him, thinking him just a little mad. But the man was immune to their pointed looks. After the horse cleared the last fence, the fan wore a smile as wide as a barn.

Big Ben walked out of the ring. The proof of his speed was on the clock. The time read 32.76 seconds.

Big Ben retired to the sidelines and stayed outside, near an entrance with Sandi and Lynn. Ian sat in the stands to see how the other riders fared. The pressure was now on them. Veterans every one, they have imaginary clocks in their heads that tell them how fast they have to go to win.

In a jumpoff, you have to rely more on instinct than on calculation. You fly and you hope. But too much speed can lead to mistakes, and not one of the four managed to go clear.

Victory went to Big Ben.

Outside the ring, Sandi had broken into her own wide smile. Someone had given her the news that Ben had won. She was patting him, but also trying to calm him down. Only a few feet away was a marching band warming up in preparation for closing ceremonies. The tubas were going *bumph-bumph bumph-bumph*, the horns were cutting loose and the snare drums were adding to the din. Ben was literally rising to the occasion, rearing up like the good guy's horse at the end of an old western.

There was so little space back there. And Ben seemed to be taking up most of it. There were uniformed musicians and flag-bearers everywhere, practically underfoot. And Ben's front feet were in the air as much as on the ground.

Sandi and Lynn were delighted by the victory, but they wanted the closing ceremony to start. By the time Ian arrived, Sandi and Lynn were both wearing worried looks.

Finally, the call came from a ring official. Sandi gave Ian a leg up on Ben, who twirled and reared. Ian settled him, and they went through the passageway back into the ring. In the centre, a suited official pinned a large yellow ribbon on Ben's martingale. A grey-blue victory blanket from Mercedes-Benz — the grand prix sponsor — was slipped onto his back.

As the band played "O Canada," the Canadian flag was slowly lowered from the rafters. At the band's first note, Ben reared once more. Then the lights in the Halle were all switched off, and the 7,500 spectators flicked on the cigarette lighters they had been handed moments before. It is a European tradition, and what a sight it is. In the spotlight was Big Ben, the ribbon on his chest, with Ian on board wearing his blazer with the red maple leaf.

The Halle had been made absolutely black, and the thousands of flickering lights encircling the ring were like a galaxy of stars on a clear summer night. All eyes were on Ian and Big Ben. Still in darkness, the audience cheered as Ian and Ben led the other riders in a victory gallop. Several spotlights followed them around the ring. The tiny lights were still flickering as the gallop ended. At the far end of the Halle, the giant computer board listed the winning rider, his nation, and his time.

Beside the number one was the name Big Ben.

★ ★ ★

Five weeks later, in December of 1989, the horse that Belgium calls its own returned to a hero's welcome. After Stuttgart, he had gone on to win the grand prix in Bordeaux, France. The two World Cup wins, in 1988 and earlier in 1989, had already made him famous in the country of his birth.

Ian was told that during a tournament in Brussels a ceremony would be held to honour Big Ben, and that the whole affair would be shown on national television. One evening, then, with Ian alone in the ring on Big Ben and not sure what to expect, an official came forward to present Ian with an oil painting of Etretat — Big Ben's father. This seemed to frighten the big gelding, and he backed and bucked and continued his little bucks for some time. Then attention turned to the in-gate. The announcer referred to a surprise in store for both Ian and Big Ben. Into the ring came a small mare who seemed oddly familiar.

Big Ben's reunion with his original family: at right, Oekie (held by her owner, Walter Konings) with Jacobus van Hooydonk and Louisa Van Looveren; at left, Etretat and his owner, Leon Phillips. (Photo courtesy Harry van Hooydonk)

It was Oekie.

"I just about died when I saw her," said Sandi, who was looking on from the side. "I looked at that mare and I said 'It's Ben.' Same colour, legs, head and neck. Same severe angles. But she was tiny."

Then came Etretat and Sandi was impressed by the well-shaped, handsome stallion.

Ben looked straight at them as they approached, all the while fixing his stare on Oekie. Ian was convinced that his horse had recognized the mare. His head was up, ears forward, and he nickered. Then came Jacobus van Hooydonk, looking dapper in a grey suit, and Louisa Van Looveren, equally elegant in a shawl and green coat. The Belgian farmers who had raised the horse they called Winston were being pulled into the limelight.

The three horses were lined up and fitted with the same dark blue victory blankets. The stallion, by now a little restless, aimed a kick at his famous son. The mare remained placid and calmly munched the carrots that someone had offered her. It was a rare moment and one not to be repeated, because in 1990 both Etretat and Oekie died quite suddenly.

No one in the Brussels stadium was untouched by the reunion. "Everyone laughed when Etretat tried to kick Ben," said Ian. "But when the ceremony was over, there wasn't a dry eye in the house. You can't imagine what a hero Big Ben is in Belgium."

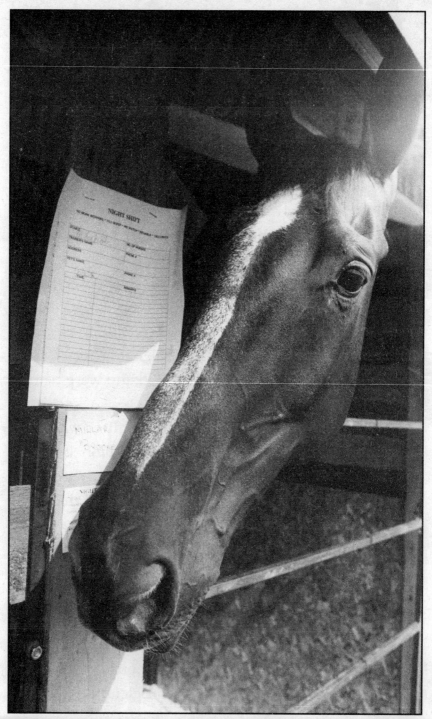

Big Ben peers out of the temporary stall that he lives in at a horse show.
(Photo by John Graydon)

8

Under the Knife

Ian and Sandi were sitting on the tack box — a blue metal trunk with Millar Brooke Farm printed in white letters on its side. They were at a stable in Tampa, Florida. It was March 10, 1990.

Papers in hand, wearing jeans and short-sleeved golf shirts, they were setting out a schedule for an upcoming competition in Ocala.

This rider and this groom have worked together a long time, and it shows. They tease each other, a clear sign of mutual trust and affection. Ian is the employer, obviously in charge, but Sandi is an employee with a powerful voice. She spends more time with Big Ben than anyone else does, and when she observes changes in his behaviour she tells Ian about them. She speaks for the horse.

It was one of those hot days that Canadians dream of in March as they look out over snow-covered fields and slushy streets. By noon, even the palm trees seemed to sag under the powerful sun.

"That's strange," said Sandi, looking over at Big Ben's stall. "He doesn't usually lie down during the day."

Ian went over to the stall, and the horse immediately rose to greet him. Ian gave his horse a pat, assured himself that all was well and returned to his seat on the trunk. *Now*, he thought, *which horse to ride in which competition. . . .*

"He just did it again," said Sandi, interrupting Ian's train of thought. She was getting a little alarmed.

"Better get the vet," Ian told her. There was a frown on his face. "This horse isn't right."

Dr. Rick Mitchell, a small but sturdy Yankee from Connecticut who worked out of a trailer on the huge Tampa showgrounds, arrived soon. By the time he got there, Big Ben was pawing the ground and circling his big double stall. The vet examined him, and then he used some medical terms that left Ian a little bewildered. The doctor didn't seem very worried, but he wasn't being terribly reassuring, either. Ian and Sandi wanted him to say something like "give the horse two Aspirin and call me in the morning."

Ian is used to being in command. He can keep a large staff motivated, keep a string of horses challenged, and keep his head when others about him are losing theirs. When things start to unravel, he can be very direct.

"Wait a minute," he said. "What am I hearing? Are you just being careful because the horse in question is Big Ben? Or is this bad and you're hiding something?"

"It's an impaction," replied Dr. Mitchell, now as forthright as Ian. "I would like to say it will pass shortly, but I can't be sure."

Over the next hour, Dr. Mitchell administered anti-inflammatory drugs. Jugs of liquid were lined up beside the horse and the fluids were injected through an intravenous line in his neck. It seemed to be working. "Hey, it's looking good," the vet pronounced before setting off to see other four-legged patients.

Sandi stayed with Ben and was chatting with two other grooms when quite suddenly, just after 5 o'clock, the big horse dropped in his stall. He fell hard, as if downed by some silent bullet. It sounded like a great bookcase had toppled forward onto the floor. Big Ben began to roll and his eyes grew wide.

Sandi was shaken, but she went right to Ben.

Come on Bennie. We've got to get you up. Come on Bennie. Walk.

Finally she did get him up and she walked him in the arena. It was the only thing she knew to do that might help. The Millar Brooke van driver, meanwhile, had gone to fetch both Ian and Dr. Mitchell. The vet came on the run. "Let's move him to the clinic at Ocala," he said, and now there was unmistakable urgency in his voice. "I hope it's just a precaution," he added. Sandi and Ian took little comfort from those words.

The clinic was an hour and a half away. Ian sat up front with the driver while Sandi monitored Big Ben in the trailer. Like all horse people, Sandi feared colic. There is almost nothing that can be done for a horse with colic, she knew. It was like having a two-year-old child suddenly become seriously ill. The child cannot understand what has gone so terribly wrong. *And Ben is like a child,* she thought. *Ben is family.*

Sandi talked to him, patted him, tried to keep him calm.

Hold on, Bennie. Hold on.

Up front, Ian was in shock. *What,* he wondered, *did we do wrong?* He was also thinking the unthinkable: that Ben's career was over, and maybe his life as well.

The surgeon at the clinic is one of the best in the United States: Dr. Don Sloan, a man who speaks slowly and deliberately, with a southern drawl.

"Do we operate?" Ian asked him when the vet had completed his examination.

Dr. Sloan replied with a question of his own. "What's your pleasure?"

"My pleasure," said Ian, "is Big Ben's bowels go clear and we compete him next week."

"I don't think so," the vet said. "It looks like surgery is necessary."

By now it was 10:00 P.M. Ian and Sandi were watching Ben in his clinic stall. They never took their eyes off him, as if somewhere, on his great chest or his head or his hocks, the answer to the puzzle would reveal itself. At one point, Ian felt strangely detached from all the emotion he was feeling. He turned to Sandi and he said, "It's like watching a kettle and waiting for it to boil, isn't it?"

The drugs being given to Big Ben were controlling the pain. Ben was not neighing, but he continued to wander in his stall — a sign of stress. At intervals, Dr. Sloan came back and asked that question of his.

"What's your pleasure, Mr. Millar?"

Ian had two key matters to ponder — the horse's career, and the horse's life. He knew that cutting into the horse's abdomen would at the very least sideline him for months. Who could say what the long-term implications were? Still, the horse's life was at stake.

Ian wanted time. As long as the horse was maintaining his composure, he considered surgery to be a last resort.

Back came Dr. Sloan, and this time he spoke more plainly. "I think surgical intervention is warranted right now," he told Ian and Sandi. "But given your reluctance, we will wait a little longer. On the other hand, we will move as soon as we see signs of him declining to a point where surgery would be jeopardized. Let's not compromise his ability to sustain the surgery."

By midnight, Ben was neither better nor worse. He offered no clues as to which way they should proceed.

"Go get some sleep," Sandi finally told Ian. "I'll stay with him." She borrowed a foal mat from someone at the clinic and curled up in front of Ben's stall. Sleep came in snatches. Every half hour she was up like a jack-in-the-box to check on Big Ben.

Oh, Bennie. Sandi would look at him and then sigh and return to her mat.

Ian was scheduled to compete in a grand prix in Ocala early the next morning. He drove all over looking for a motel and finally found one at 2 o'clock in the morning. It looked rough around the edges but at least it had a phone. The rest of the Millar family, Lynn, Jonathon and Amy, had been at Disney World all day and earlier in the evening Ian had managed to track down Lynn to tell her the bad news. Now he called her again to describe the holding pattern that

Big Ben seemed to be in. Then Ian put his head down. Fitfully, he slept.

But not for long. At 6:30 A.M. the phone rang. Ian had it in his hands before the second ring. In that drawl of his, Dr. Sloan used a medical phrase.

"I'm getting ready to cut on your horse," he said.

"Don't!" said Ian. "I'll be right there."

When Ian next saw Ben, a few minutes later, he scarcely recognized him. The horse looked physically depressed. Ian could see how much he had deteriorated. And yet he still found it hard to believe that all this was happening. He had truly thought that the morning call would be to say, 'Come get your horse. He's fine now. You can jump him in the ring next week.' Now they were out of options. Surgery, or Ben would die.

While veterinary staff prepared for surgery, Ian called Lynn, who rushed to the clinic. When Lynn got there, the great emotion that had been welling up inside Sandi finally burst. She had not shed one tear until that moment; now the tears were falling and they would not stop.

Ian went into the stall and gave Ben a pat on the neck. "See you later, big boy," he said to his horse, and then he stepped back out. Sandi, Ian and Lynn stood there, looking through the glass window of the clinic stall. Their eyes glistened with tears, they were tired and dazed, and none of them was sure they would see Big Ben alive again.

The surgery went well. Dr. Sloan located the blockage that was causing all the trouble, injected it with salt, and managed to move it along. There was no need to cut into the intestine. In colic surgery, the simpler the better.

Sandi maintained her vigil in front of Ben's stall as he recovered. "It's OK," staff at the clinic assured her. "You can go home." They were not used to having grooms camped out in front of stalls. But she would not go.

The Ocala clinic deals almost exclusively with thoroughbred horses. The name Big Ben meant nothing there.

"He's a champion horse," Sandi informed the staff.

"Do you have any idea," one bemused doctor told her, "how many people tell us their sick horses are champions?"

But when get-well cards began to arrive at the clinic, when reporters were found trying to sneak into the barn and the telephone rang incessantly, staff got the idea that Big Ben was a special horse, all right.

Sandi stayed rooted to the spot for two days. Millar Brooke staff brought food and changes of clothing to her.

Right after the operation, Ben looked awful. He was disoriented, lost. At one point he peered through the glass windows of the stall and caught sight of Sandi. He nickered at her. It was a good sign.

The morning of the operation, Ian had somehow managed to pull himself together and ride in the Ocala tournament on other Millar Brooke horses. When he got back to the clinic, he got good news and bad news. The good news concerned the surgery and how well it had gone. The bad news, for Ian, concerned all the complications that can follow such surgery.

"You're not even close to being out of the woods yet," said Dr. Sloan. "Not for six weeks anyway."

The plan of recovery — written out in great detail by Dr. Sloan — involved keeping the horse moving. Constant light exercise was the prescription. For weeks, Sandi walked him every day. Then she walked him with a rider on board. Clinic staff were astonished at how well and how quickly Big Ben recuperated. The consensus was that his superb physical condition was speeding recovery along at an incredible pace. But would he be the same Ben in the show ring?

A few weeks later, Ian was able to ride him for the first time. Big Ben was as excited as Sandi had ever seen him. Ian prepared himself as a rodeo rider would for a bucking bronco.

Exactly three months after surgery, Big Ben went back into the ring for his first grand prix at the Spruce Meadows Nationals. The people of Calgary hold a special place in their hearts for Big Ben, and they cheered him long and loud when he trotted out the

For weeks after his attack of colic, Sandi walked Big Ben every day. (Photo by Jayne Huddleston)

first time early in the week. When he won the grand prix a few days later, they were ecstatic.

Big Ben went on to four grand prix victories that year. In Nations' Cup competitions — team events that pit riders of various countries against each other — he went clear both rounds in New Jersey, both rounds in Toronto, and clear in each jumpoff.

Ben was back, all right. That year, 1990, the year of his first colic operation, he was the Canadian champion. The horse that had been laid low had rebounded mightily, apparently stronger than ever.

It has been the story of his life.

Big Ben bounced back from colic surgery in 1990 to become Canadian champion that year. (Photo by Jayne Huddleston)

9

On the Comeback Trail

In 1990, Big Ben had survived colic — that terrible scourge of horses — and the year had ended on a triumphant note. But in January of 1991, colic struck Big Ben yet again. It took the skill of the surgical team at the University of Guelph veterinary clinic to save his life.

Back at Millar Brooke, everyone felt relief that he had survived. But the horse's rider and the horse's groom were both thinking the same thing. *Big Ben is fifteen years old now, and we cannot expect an older horse to endure two colic operations and still perform like a champion in the ring.*

Other trainers and riders were convinced that the great career had come to a tragic halt. Show jumpers are high-performance athletes. Injury can diminish them physically. Age can dull the spirit. Their time to shine in the show ring is unmercifully short. Big Ben, everyone said, was past his prime anyway. But now two major operations, only ten months apart? Nope. Put him out to pasture.

"We figured for sure his career was over," Ian says. "No one was saying it too much around Millar Brooke. But we were thinking it." When people asked him about it, Ian put on a brave face. Big Ben would come back, he told reporters and other riders. The horse had done it before and he would do it again.

For almost two months after the second surgery, Sandi just walked him every day. His diet was changed in an attempt to keep his bowels from acting up again. In February, Ian decided to take him south to Florida. Ontario can be unrelentingly cold and grey in February. Perhaps the warm sun would cheer Big Ben and speed up the healing process.

Whether it was the sun or Big Ben's remarkable constitution, he did heal quickly. The spring came back into his step. He was eager to get back to work. Ian began to ride him. Within a month, he was ready for competition.

This was already an amazing recovery, but the

sceptics would only be convinced if he returned to his old form. In show jumping, past performance counts for little. Until he won again, Big Ben would be yesterday's horse.

Early in April of 1991, Big Ben returned to the ring. He looked refreshed. It was as if he had been away on a three-month holiday, not battling back from abdominal surgery. "Never underestimate me," this magnificent Belgian gelding seemed to be saying.

Sandi has a theory that the colic surgeries, though horrible, were actually a blessing in disguise. For while Big Ben recovered, he got time off. The workaholic horse was forced to rest, and each time he returned to the ring rejuvenated and went on to record banner years. Ian takes a different view: he believes the horse would have accomplished what he did in any case, and he wonders how many other competitions Big Ben might have won in the six months he was sidelined.

That June, Big Ben faced the stiffest possible test of his resilience. The gruelling derby at Spruce Meadows features twenty-three jumps — almost twice as many as in normal competitions — and these include a ditch aptly named "the devil's dike" and a perilously long and steep bank. Big Ben had won the derby in 1986, 1987 and 1988. In 1989 he came in second to El Futuro, another of Ian's horses. His derby record was phenomenal. But could he do it again?

Ian gives Big Ben a quick pat on the neck during their victory gallop at Spruce Meadows. (Photo by Shawn Hamilton/Clix)

Ian and Ben jumped last, so Ian could watch the course confound every horse and rider combination. The derby is not for the faint of heart.

But Ben leapt every fence cleanly, and when Ian pulled up at the in-gate he wore a look on his face of both joy and disbelief.

Jayne Huddleston, an equestrian journalist, remembers the moment perfectly. "Ian shook his head and he looked at me and said, 'He's quite a man, isn't he?' That, to me, was one of the really miraculous wins in Big Ben's life. I know of horses that took a year to recover from colic. I've seen many horses *not* come back from colic. That derby win was a milestone."

Two months later, Big Ben challenged for the grand prix at the Spruce Meadows Masters in Calgary — the richest show jumping event in the world and the one that every great rider hates to miss.

Whenever Ian competed with Big Ben that week, the crowd cheered warmly. They were the kind of cheers bestowed on a great athlete who has always made it look easy, but whose greatness is perhaps more in the past than in the present or future. Everyone in that crowd knew of the colic operations and while they hoped that Big Ben might win — and the derby proved he could — they no longer expected it.

The fans at Spruce Meadows are well-informed. They realize that show jumping asks a lot of both horse and rider. The burden on the rider is as much mental as physical, and is therefore often overlooked by a spectator seeing the sport for the first time. Someone once likened show jumping to a chess match played at a frenzied pace. As in chess, every bad move will cost you. A rider in the show ring has to think every bit as fast as the horse beneath him or her is moving.

When Ian rode Big Ben into the ring early that week at Spruce Meadows, it was business as usual, and that meant he had a lot on his mind:

1. *Where to go.* Twelve or so numbered jumps must be taken in order in about eighty seconds. This looks simple from the stands. It is not. Courses snake crazily left and right and back again and a one-second pause to get his bearings will cost Ian a victory. Jump the fences in the wrong order and you are disqualified. Riders do get lost on course.

2. *How to go.* In a canter, a controlled gallop, Ian strives to guide Big Ben economically to a precise spot at the base of each jump — mere centimetres matter. So Ian walks the course before the competition and measures the number of horse strides between jumps. Each distance is different, so he keeps those numbers in his head. From jump 1 to jump 2, six strides; jump 2 to jump 3, four and a half strides, and so on. And there is one more thing to consider: sometimes a competition features a jumpoff in which finalists race against the clock over a shortened

version of the course. Ian had better have that map and its stride lengths memorized too. Big Ben needs all that information.

3. *His partner.* Ian must keep Big Ben focused. The crowd, banners, fences with optical illusions, water jumps — all these can distract him. Course designers have countless tricks to bewilder horses. That is why Ian spends hundreds of hours each year schooling Big Ben. In the ring, Big Ben has his work cut out for him: he is changing leads, changing speeds, turning on a dime, staying balanced, maintaining his form right to the last fence. The messages from Ian's legs, seat and hands are constant and the horse must respond instantly.

Big Ben needs all his power to leap these high fences at Spruce Meadows — the verticals, the oxers or combinations, the triple bar jumps. He also needs courage and confidence, as does Ian. If Ian keeps all the numbers straight in his head, if Big Ben trusts him, if the dozen or so variables in this horse-human team click just right, they might go clear. They might win. They might take your breath away.

Spruce Meadows, located just south of Calgary, is an extraordinary place. Only two other show jumping grounds in the world — Aachen in Germany and Hickstead in England — can compare with it. In every way, the facility is world class. Three major competitions are held on its sprawling grounds each summer, but the one that draws the best riders and horses in the world is the Spruce Meadows Masters, held in September.

Two hundred riders and 400 horses come — from England, France, Germany, Switzerland, Austria, Ireland, Mexico, Holland and the United States. On the last day of the five-day competition, grand prix day, up to 46,000 fans fill the stands to watch the jumping in the international ring. Television coverage beams the event to as many as twenty-six countries. The prize money for the week tops $2 million, and the winner of the grand prix takes home no less than $225,000. The fences are high, the course always tough. It brings out the best and the worst in horse and rider.

On the day before the grand prix, the Nations' Cup competition is held. This team event pits four riders from each nation against one another. The team with the fewest faults wins. Riders will often use their so-called "second" horses and rest their top mounts, saving the better horses for the far more lucrative grand prix on Sunday. Ian almost never does that. Big Ben competed for Canada that Saturday and went two rounds without a fault, the only horse to do so.

But would he be too tired now for the grand prix? The next day was cool and bright, with the course still wet from morning rain. In round one, Ian and Big Ben went clear. They had a close call at a water jump, avoiding the tape by only a fraction of an inch. Had they touched the tape, they would have incurred faults. Of thirty-nine horse and rider combinations, only twelve went on to the second round and only three of those had gone clear.

In the ensuing second round, Ian and Ben needed a clear round to win. The crowd gave them a rousing send-off, so loud that Ian waited almost a full minute before setting out on the course. Big Ben was sailing along, ears perked, and the crowd tensed, then cheered, at every fence. At the fourth-last jump, Big Ben rattled the rail.

"There is often a moment during a competition," says Ian, "when the horse's hooves touch the rail. You hear that noise, and then you hear a thud." That's the sound of the rail hitting the ground. For Ian, it is also the sound of prize money going down the drain. That day, Ian heard the *clunk* of hoof on rail and as he rode on to the next jump he listened. First he heard gasps — a sign that the rail was wobbling and perhaps on its way down. Then he heard cheers — the rail had stayed up. Ian then did something he rarely does: he looked back, just to make sure, as they rode on to the next jump.

Colic times two, that was bad luck. But a rail that goes *clunk* and then bounces neatly back into the cups, this was *good* luck. And Big Ben had some coming to him. At the second-last jump, the crowd sighed again when Big Ben caused the vertical to shiver ever so slightly but then he sailed high over the last oxer. The applause erupted and the crowd stood in celebration.

For the second time in his career, Big Ben had won this prestigious event. No other horse and rider combination had ever won the Spruce Meadows Masters twice. Big Ben won it by going two rounds without a fault, just a day after performing the same feat in the Nations' Cup.

The tradition at Spruce Meadows is the same as at all tournaments: winning horses are lined up in the ring for a presentation ceremony. Horse and rider face the stands while ribbons are awarded. But at the Masters the spectators stick around through these formalities, waiting to hear from the winner of this most coveted prize.

Big Ben had been pulling in crowds at Spruce Meadows for eight years and Calgarians love him. Ian Millar spent seven years of his youth living in Alberta: that would make him almost a home-town boy. The crowd rose and clapped, for the home team had won. The comeback trail for Big Ben had ended in glory.

A large red ribbon was pinned on Big Ben's martingale. The red victory blanket with the name of the sponsor emblazoned on it was slipped over his back. Ian dismounted and said a few words into a microphone. He was feeling the tremendous sense of elation that great victory always brings, but he was also remembering all the anguish that his horse had endured over the past eighteen months. Emotion crept into his voice as he spoke.

"I want to make sure," he told the hushed spectators as he gestured towards Big Ben, "that everyone knows who the true champion is today and that's this magnificent horse." Then he threw his helmet into the air and wiped away a tear before cantering Big Ben around the ring, the other horses following behind like the bows on the tail of a high-flying kite.

One of the trailers in which Big Ben has travelled many miles. (Photo by Jayne Huddleston)

10

Terror On the Highway

The horse van — a handsome grey and blue trailer with sliding green-tinted windows high on its sides — was rolling along the highway forty kilometres east of Saskatoon, Saskatchewan. Midnight was approaching. Traffic was light.

Sandi sat up front with the driver, a man named Ken Armstrong. Her tennis shoes were off, her feet bare, as she drifted between sleep and wakefulness. The tires hummed on the wet pavement, for it was raining hard, and the truck's heater was steadily blowing warm air to fend off the cold outside. The rocking of the big rig made for a rough sort of cradle. Sandi is accustomed to catching snatches of sleep in odd places: on a cot by Big Ben's stall at tournaments, on a foaling mat at a vet clinic, in a truck heading west along a dark stretch of highway.

Eight horses were in the van that night of May 24, 1992. Four of them were from Millar Brooke Farm — Big Ben, a stallion named Winchester, Future Vision, and a promising young horse called Baarlo. The Dutch trainer Emile Hendrix, who had found Big Ben for Ian, had discovered this one too. Ian had named him after Emile's home town in Holland. Some were already calling Baarlo the next Big Ben.

Big Ben was in his accustomed position behind the driver's seat. That spot offers the most comfortable ride. Whatever comfort is to be had on a fifty-seven hour trek across the country, Big Ben is the one who gets it. The van was part of a convoy: several vehicles with grooms inside were right behind, and ten minutes farther back were two other horse vans carrying the mounts of Canadian riders Mario Deslauriers and Beth Underhill.

The destination that night was Edmonton, to be followed by another week-long tournament in Calgary, and then back home again to southeastern Ontario. It is a long time for a horse to spend on the road, but it is unavoidable. Air travel would make more sense and take a lot less out of the horses. But some years ago, the one airline in Canada that offered the service declared it unprofitable and cancelled it.

That explains why Big Ben is on the highway a lot every year. West to Alberta, east to Nova Scotia and Quebec, south to Florida, New York State and perhaps Arizona or California.

"Hey," Ken said suddenly, and so loud it woke Sandi up. "That guy's lights are on my side of the road!"

There was no mistake. Another set of lights was locked on theirs. Another vehicle was hurtling directly towards them at 100 kilometres an hour.

It all happened in seconds, yet the chain of events seemed, for Sandi, to unfold in agonizingly slow motion. The braking of the horse van. The futile attempt to swerve and miss the oncoming vehicle. The horrible sounds: the other vehicle exploding into flames on impact, glass breaking and metal buckling as the horse van's front axle received the blow. The crippled van out of control, sliding sideways down the highway, then heading into the ditch and flopping, ever so slowly, onto its right side.

Sandi's heart was pounding and would not stop. Instinct would have to guide her now, because her world had literally been turned upside down.

"Are you OK?" she asked when the horse van had finally come to a shuddering halt. Gravity pressed her against the side window. Had she been able to roll the window down, Sandi would have found her face in prairie dirt.

"I think so," Ken said. "But my legs . . . they're pinned. I can't move them. You better go see about the horses. I'm OK until help comes."

With both rig and van lying on their sides, even getting the driver's-side door open was a task. Sandi had to crawl over Ken, then push the door up and hold it open so she could ease her body out. The heavy door was now like a submarine hatch — if she let go of it, it would come crashing back down on top of her.

About a hundred metres behind, the other vehicle was engulfed in flames. It was like a war scene. The fire was making an awful crackling sound and a small roar was coming from somewhere.

In her bare feet, the rain pelting down and getting in her eyes, Sandi scrambled over the side of the van and found the door to the rear where the horses were. With strength she hardly knew she possessed, she got the heavy side door open and lifted it up.

Some lights were still on inside the van. Sandi was looking down as if into the hold of some great ship at sea. The wooden beams that normally stood upright were now just so many horizontal pick-up sticks, some bent and broken. Beneath them were horses.

"Ben!" she screamed. "Ben!"

Gripped by terror, the horses were struggling to find footing on the metal sides of the van. With their metal shoes, they kept sliding back down again. It was an agonizing thing to watch. They were neighing unceasingly and crashing around down there like loose cargo in the hold of a ship during a storm. Like the others, Big Ben was struggling to stand.

Sandi jumped down and raced around to the back of the van. *Get the horses out,* she was thinking. *Must get them out.*

But the back door was jammed shut.

The two Millar Brooke grooms travelling in the truck behind had themselves come perilously close to hitting both the other vehicle, a mini-van, and the front axle of the horse van, which had been sheared off in the collision. Fighting shock, they rushed to the trailer and tried to help Sandi. Now soaked to the skin, she felt completely helpless. The three of them could do little but wait for help. One flagged down a driver who agreed to rush to the nearest phone and call for police, ambulances and fire trucks.

There was glass all over the road, but somehow, Sandi's bare feet were never cut as she circled the trailer. At one point, she and the others thought about trying to get the driver out of the mini-van. But the flames and the heat drove them back.

Each time Sandi scrambled up onto the side of the trailer to look inside, the same gruesome sight greeted her. Horses frantically trying to stand, succeeding for a time, then losing their footing. Up and down they went, a mad merry-go-round. One horse at the back of the van, Tesa, had died instantly from the impact, and the smell of spilled blood added to the horses' terror. Eventually, the seven remaining horses went into shock and stopped calling out. Baarlo had fallen down and was kept pinned under the hooves of another horse, Gusty Monroe.

Finally, their batteries spent, the remaining lights inside the van went out. The horses were in darkness.

The other horse vans and grooms arrived on the scene ten minutes after the accident They saw the flaming mini-van and stopped to help, but they were unaware of the horse van in the ditch down the road. When they saw it, they assumed that a farmer had suffered a mishap and one of them went ahead to investigate. It was only when she came running back out of the darkness that it hit the rest of them.

"Ian's horses are trapped!" the groom screamed. They grabbed flashlights and went running down the side of the road towards the van. Even before they got there they could see the lone figure of Sandi Patterson standing on top of the van and struggling to keep the door open. The high beams of a passing truck threw a blinding white light on the scene. As the diesel swept past, the rush of air sucked at their clothing. Then it grew quiet again. From her terrible perch, Sandi looked into the flashlights' glare and frantically pleaded for help.

When the ambulance drivers and firefighters got

there half an hour later, they attended to the casualties. The driver of the mini-van was dead. Ken Armstrong was freed from the horse van and taken away to hospital.

Attention now turned to the exhausted but still wide-eyed horses. When horses are involved in highway accidents, it is often not the crash itself that kills them. They flee the wreckage and are cut down by oncoming cars and trucks. Traffic continued to roar by the stricken van. How, then, to get the horses out safely with the back door jammed shut?

By this time, Big Ben had used his head like a pile driver to make a hole in the van's side — now its roof. He had a bad cut over his right eye, either from slamming his head into the metal or from the accident itself.

Get the horses out. Get them out. It was Sandi's only thought.

She and the others used a crowbar and their bare hands to make holes in what had once been the roof of the van. Like people possessed, they tore at the metal to get at the horses. Eventually, they peeled back the roof near the front and made a hole wide enough for the horses to scramble out. When they shone in their flashlights, they could see Big Ben in a corner. They got him up and out first. The grooms hastily put bridles and leads on horses that were not already wearing them. Future Vision came out next, then the others.

At some earlier point in the scrambling, Gusty Monroe and Baarlo had switched places. Baarlo now stood on top of Gusty, who moaned every time Baarlo shifted his weight. When the grooms finally freed them, Gusty emerged covered in blood, most of it from wounds to his neck; his knee was also torn open to the bone.

Grooms held most of the horses but a few firefighters in heavy coats and fire hats, who had never been close to a horse in their lives, were given the task of holding onto the bridles of champions. One awestruck firefighter was given Baarlo.

"He may spook," Sandi instructed him. "If he goes back, you go back with him."

But the seven horses still alive seemed so relieved to be out and so spent from their struggle that none had the energy to object to the trucks whistling by bare metres away. From an emergency trunk in the van, Sandi and the others got blankets and put them over the horses. At that point, one groom noticed that Sandi was still barefoot and brought her a spare pair of shoes.

As usual, a little good luck came with the bad. Saskatoon has the best equine clinic in western Canada. Alerted to the terrible accident, vets there set up a makeshift hospital unit so they could quickly establish which horses were most badly hurt and treat them first. Had the accident occurred in northern Ontario, a day away from expert veterinary help, the outcome might have been quite different.

But before the vets could get to work, the battered horses had to be brought to them. The driver of the second van returned to the accident scene after first dropping off his own horses at the Rusty Spurs Equestrian Centre. Sympathetic people there had generously cleared a section of their barn. The emptied van was then used to transport the seven exhausted horses to the clinic.

By now an hour and a half had elapsed. When the horses were finally packed away in the van and sent off, and the adrenalin had stopped coursing through the veins of the grooms, they had to face the reality of what had happened. Some wept in the rain. Some slipped away in the dark and were sick to their stomachs. One became hysterical. They would all have nightmares for months.

One of the two Millar Brooke grooms who had been travelling right behind in a truck was a young girl. The memory of that night has never left her. When the accident occurred, a song had been playing on the truck radio. Whenever she heard that song in the months to come, she wept uncontrollably.

At the clinic, veterinarians drew up the injury list. It was not short. Big Ben required stitches over his eye and he had a graze on his nose and cuts on his legs. Gusty suffered an eight-inch cut in the knee from broken glass. Future Vision, a stalwart in the Millar Brooke stable, had one hock cut badly by

Some of the other horses in the highway accident. Top: Future Vision (with Ian Millar). Bottom left: Gusty Monroe (with Sarah Watt, his owner) took almost a year to recover from his injuries, but has returned to form. Bottom right: Like Big Ben, Winchester went right back to competition. Sadly, he died of a heart attack one year later. (Photos by Jayne Huddleston)

broken glass. Poor Baarlo, so long pinned, appeared to suffer only superficial cuts and bruises, but even a year later he had not recovered. Some mysterious ailment continued to afflict his back, and no amount of massage, acupuncture or chiropractic manipulation seemed to work. He finally returned to the show ring in California early in 1994.

The horses were rested for a week at the stable. None jumped at the Edmonton tournament. A week or so later, when they were taken to Calgary, they practically bolted out of the trailer. The memory of what had happened was still fresh in their minds. For months afterwards, the horses were spooky in and around horse trailers.

Only two horses bounced right back — Winchester and Big Ben. It seemed the old pros knew they were at Spruce Meadows and had a job to do. Yet they had clearly been affected by the accident. In the exercise rings, Ian could feel that the accident ten days before had taken some of the wind out of Big Ben's sails. The old enthusiasm seemed gone.

But the first day in the warmup ring near the competition area revealed a different horse. The practices had gone badly, but now it was game time, and Big Ben knew it. He reared and twirled like a rodeo horse. "He was a hazard to ride," Ian said later, "shying, spooking and spinning around." Ian entered Big Ben in three classes that week and won all three, including a grand prix — Ian's 100th.

In those three events, Big Ben recorded five clear rounds, including two in the grand prix on Saturday. Then he capped the perfect week by winning the notoriously gruelling derby. The course is about 930 metres long — nearly twice as long as the grand prix course.

When a horse and rider combination is completely defeated by a course, with fences flying and the horse going down, riders call it "crashing and burning." There was a lot of crashing and burning at Spruce Meadows in June of 1992. Only one horse of the twenty-three entered managed the derby course without a fault.

Big Ben.

He looked slightly war-weary as Ian galloped him to celebrate the derby victory, with the stitches over his eye still in place. But there was nothing at all wrong with his heart. Big Ben had now won the derby an unprecedented five times.

His performance that day seemed almost playful. He was the last to go and as he continued to jump cleanly, the crowd cheered every leap. Ever the sentimental favourite at Spruce Meadows, Big Ben had acquired hero status after rebounding from the two colic surgeries and now this latest assault, the highway accident.

A closeup photograph of Sandi embracing Big Ben had recently appeared on the front page of the *Calgary Herald*. "Big Ben is a survivor," the headline read. As the derby unfolded, everyone was pulling for him.

At the water jump, the crowd cheered louder still. Suddenly, despite the taxing nature of this competition, Ian had more — not less — horse on his hands. The louder the crowd cheered, the higher Big Ben jumped. Ian thought, *He's blowing them away. He's playing to the crowd.*

A *Calgary Herald* writer afterwards laid on the praise. He called Ian and Big Ben "a little slice of heaven on earth":

> As flawless as clean glass.
>
> They didn't just jump over obstacles. They floated over them. They soared where others crashed. Their grace and power were so extraordinary they had the record crowd at Spruce Meadows standing on their feet and applauding the moment.

The writer wondered if this might be the year for that Olympic medal that had long eluded Big Ben. Unfortunately, it was not to be. Ian and Ben picked the 1992 Olympic Games in Barcelona, Spain to do some rare crashing and burning of their own. They came in fifty-fourth.

That set off yet more predictions. The horse had finally had enough. After almost a decade of jumping, Big Ben was headed for the paddock. The 1993 show jumping circuit would be one long retirement party for Big Ben. He would compete only in some light classes here and there so his admirers could see him one more time. And again, the experts were wrong.

The derby, the dreaded derby at Spruce Meadows — that stiff test of endurance and courage — still belonged to Ben. In June of '93, he won it for the third consecutive year, and for the sixth time in his career. No other horse has come close to matching that achievement. Big Ben took every jump in the derby before knocking down the very last one. This forced a jumpoff against two other horses, which he narrowly won.

In the fall of 1993, Big Ben continued to win: two second-place ribbons at the Atlantic Winter Fair in Halifax, double-clear rounds at the Nations' Cup event in New Jersey, and two first-place results against stiff international competition at the Royal Winter Fair in Toronto.

How does he do it? How does this senior citizen of a horse keep his coltish spirit?

"It's unbelievable," said Ian after the derby win in '93. "He has learned to be an extremely efficient athlete. He has learned to do what he does with a minimum of physical and mental stress. In the derby, he just used a little less energy than other horses going around that course."

"He has no weakness," Ian would say later. "His only enemy now is time."

11

In the Eyes of the Beholder

In white T-shirt, blue jeans and yellow chaps, Grant Cashmore rode Big Ben in a long narrow field. The backdrop was a fence-line of trees, all green but for the odd leaf touched by gold during these last days of August, 1993. At a glance you could see that this young man and this long-in-the-tooth horse understood one another.

Tanned and freckled, his lips a little sunburned, Grant looked fit and strong, the laid-back sort who prefers paddocks and the company of horses to an office. Grant is from New Zealand, but for the past several months he had been at Millar Brooke Farm watching and learning about riding grand prix horses from Ian Millar. He also had the chance to exercise Big Ben, both at the farm and on the road at competitions such as this one: the Collingwood Horse Show, not far from Toronto.

The light filtering through the thunder clouds brought out the deep red colour in Big Ben's tail and mane. The mane rippled in the wind; the tail swirled, but it was hard to tell from the sidelines whether this was due to flies or bad temper. At the field's corners, Big Ben would shift out of his big striding walk and ease into a trot before coming down to a walk again.

Most of the spectators were in the bleachers watching the jumping in the grand prix ring. But as always at horse shows, there was much to see beyond the ring for those who love horses. Some looked with interest upon the schooling and conditioning exercises, much as serious baseball fans watch batting practice before a game.

Among this bunch was a two-year-old boy walking with his mother by the one-board, waist-high fence that separated the horses and riders in the exercise area from onlookers. Suddenly the child's eyes grew wide. He pointed and yelled, "Big Ben! Big Ben!" Somehow this little boy had come not only to have a favourite horse but to pick him out of a dozen others.

When the ride was over, Sandi came by to take Big Ben back to his stall. Grant stuck around to watch horses and riders going over practice jumps just behind the entrance to the ring. As he did this, he talked about the horse he had just been riding and the great affection that people, especially young people, bestow on him.

"I walk Big Ben at horse shows, and I remember being at the Ottawa show a few weeks ago. I never saw anything like it. The kids were all around him. 'Can I pat him?' they would ask. 'Can I hop on him?'" Grant laughed heartily at the notion. "I'd never seen such strong feeling for an animal."

Over the years, Millar Brooke Farm has tried to accommodate several parents whose children were dying of cancer. Among these children's last wishes was the chance to see their hero, Big Ben. One girl actually got up on his back in Calgary; others were content to visit his stall at Millar Brooke and pat him.

The horse seems to inspire extraordinary feeling, and not just in children. In October of 1992, twenty-nine-year-old Holly MacIntyre of Sydney, Nova Scotia drove 400 kilometres to watch the horse compete in Halifax at the Atlantic Winter Fair. Not a rider but mad about horses all the same, she had been following Big Ben's career since 1986. She hoped to pat him but the crowds around him at Exhibition Park in Halifax were always too thick.

"Leave it with me," said her husband, a CBC-TV

In 1987, a terminally ill teenager chose a ride on Big Ben as her last wish. (Photo by Jayne Huddleston)

employee who had a surprise in mind and the contacts to pull it off. Some time later Holly, standing in the walkway at ringside, noticed a television camera trained on her. When someone nearby asked her to turn around, she found herself face to face with a very familiar, very large horse. The camera caught Holly bursting into tears, but then she calmed herself, took the sugar that Sandi offered her and fed it to Big Ben while she explained to the television audience her great love for the horse.

"What struck me was how he held his head," Holly said later. "Like he was royalty. But he was very gentle as he took the sugar. And then later, during the competition, he made a turn like you would not believe, and he won the class. He does give his all."

Another fan, a ninety-one-year-old woman from St. George, New Brunswick, wrote Ian in September of 1992 with an odd request. She wanted some hair from Big Ben's mane and tail. "Then I can say," she explained, "that I own one ten-millionth share of him. I will tie the hair with a blue ribbon and attach it to Big Ben's picture. Please do an old wrinkled, swayback broken-down old mare (me) this last favour."

Fans write Big Ben to ask for his hoofprint autograph. Sandi often obliges by dabbing the horse's shoe with hoof oil and having him press down on blank paper.

Young people who come around to see Big Ben at

tournaments are often riders themselves, and all of them want to know: What's it like to ride him? Does he feel different from other horses? In Grant Cashmore's words:

"He's a horse who sizes you up really quickly. The first time I rode him he wouldn't trot for me. I mean, he would trot, but it took ten strides before he would do it. Once you get his respect, he's fine. He's very brainy. If I don't tell him to do something, he'll go along and do his own thing. He has great personality. He's like a human. If he can get away with something, he will.

"What you feel when you ride him is his power. *Major* power. He has a beautiful canter. He's really well schooled. I've never met a horse like him, one who knows when he's going into the ring and when he's just going out for a walk. He's the smartest horse I've ever ridden. But not smart and dirty."

What Grant meant by smart and dirty is that some horses are both intelligent and mean. Ben is not a mean character, but he is a very smart one.

"The other day I was riding him out here," Grant pointed back to the field where he had just been, "and all of a sudden he just stopped. There was a fly on his head. And he turned his head to look back at me, as if to say, 'Grant, would you swat that fly from my head, please?'

"He certainly doesn't feel or look like a seventeen-year-old horse," the young rider said. "He feels like a twelve-year-old. There's still plenty of power there. It's been a real privilege to ride him."

The big sky here on the shores of Georgian Bay looked nasty this day: dark clouds were scudding overhead and the show announcer spoke of a severe weather warning. Grooms were advised to secure the flaps on the horse tents and to consider digging trenches to divert the heavy rain that was predicted. Each rider had been allocated stalls, with that farm's name clearly marked on personalized tent flaps, on folding chairs and on tack boxes. By Big Ben's stall sat a blue tack box with chrome trim and the letters MBF in the middle.

The Collingwood Horse Show had the relaxed feel of a county fair, the kind of place where dairy princesses make appearances and frog-jumping contests are announced. The centrepiece of the tournament was the grand prix ring, flanked on the west and south by bleachers. To the east was a hunter ring, where riders and horses vaulted lower fences and were also judged on their form.

In the afternoon, Ian had three horses in one competition: Big Ben, Future Vision and Lonesome Dove. All three made it into the nine-horse jumpoff, but Big Ben seemed to be off his usual form. He was a bit sharper in the jumpoff, but even then he rapped the first fence hard without knocking it down. This seemed to wake him up. In the end, Future Vision took the red ribbon, edging out Big Ben by a few tenths of a second, with Lonesome Dove further down the list.

Ian admitted afterwards that Big Ben seemed "a little sluggish" at first, although he was fine in the jumpoff.

While Ian rode into the ring to collect his ribbons, Sandi walked back to the Millar Brooke Farm stalls. She wore sunglasses, turquoise shorts and a rose-coloured golf shirt. Over her shoulder was slung some tack and in her belt was tucked a small towel used to give Ian's boots and stirrups a wipe before he enters the ring. Behind her, on a lead, was Big Ben. To anyone who frequents summer show jumping tournaments, it is a familiar sight.

When it was suggested to Sandi that the horse didn't seem to be his old self in the ring, she would have none of it. "It's early in the week," she replied. "I'm sure he'll be right on form for the weekend."

By now the sun had reappeared, the wind had calmed and rain no longer threatened. Ian Millar was lunging Future Vision in front of his stalls. Using voice commands backed up by a long light whip, he had the saddled horse walk and trot in a wide circle. Then Ian would stop him, and start him up again. When he was done, Ian casually asked another rider if he had seen a certain film in which a character tries to mount a horse the way they do in westerns — a flying leap from behind. In the film, a comedy, the horse bolts and the rider lands on his fanny. "I want to try that," Ian said, straight-faced, before pacing out six steps behind Future Vision. "Don't do it, Ian," the other rider pleaded. Ian did not, of course, but he had the other rider convinced he would.

Big Ben, meanwhile, was back in his stall. Sandi took an adjustable wrench out of the tack box to remove his caulks — "Ben's running shoes" she always calls these small bolts screwed into the hooves to improve traction. But the horse kept using one leg to dust off a fly or two on his belly, making Sandi's job more difficult.

"Ben, I see the flies," she told him. "They're not that bad." And then he would lift his hoof to delicately shoo another one. "*Bennnnnnnnnn.*"

Across the way, Canadian rider Harold Chopping had work to do around his own corner of the horse-tent village. He was all in black — jet-black hair, black shirt and dark sunglasses — but his manner was cheery as he answered questions about Big Ben.

"I always thought he was a special horse," Harold began. "When he went into the ring and things *had* to work out, I rarely saw him fail. It was very exciting to be on Nations' Cup teams with Big Ben. A horse like that anchors the team. No matter the score, you always have a pair of cleans and a better chance. He's won a lot, that one," said Harold, looking over at Big Ben's stall. "But when you're competing against him you always had a sinking feeling if he went into the ring after you did.

"It comes down to heart and the horse's desire to compete. That one" — and once more Harold shot an affectionate glance in Big Ben's direction — "loves to compete."

A mix of veteran grand prix riders, up-and-comers, and trainers who have been around the block was gathered at the Collingwood Horse Show. All of them spoke of Big Ben with much fondness and not a little awe.

Around the corner from Harold Chopping was Beth Underhill, a young blond rider whose mount is a striking black New Zealand-bred horse called Monopoly. Asked what makes Big Ben special, she began haltingly, but then warmed to the task. "I have never seen a horse who understands competition the way he does," she said. "He's a big horse but he seems to grow before your eyes in the ring. And for the size of him, he's very adjustable. He's just as comfortable opening his stride in a gallop at Spruce Meadows as he is shortening stride. He can jump on an angle, nip back at big oxers. He's as comfortable indoors as outdoors."

Looking for words to explain all the affection for the horse, Beth looked over to the ring for an instant and seemed to find them there. "He has this overwhelming presence. Maybe that explains why kids love him. People recognize that he's a great athlete and they're very interested in him. The deep feeling that Ian and Sandi have for him — everyone else in the show jumping world appreciates that. It's special. We'll miss him when he goes."

Back at Big Ben's stall, some minor horse trading was underway. Andrea Wernham, a fourteen-year-old from London, Ontario, struck a deal with Sandi. Andrea decorates T-shirts with the names of famous horses — Big Ben among them, of course — and sells them at tournaments. She had offered one to Sandi in exchange for horseshoes worn by Big Ben and Lonesome Dove.

"I like the way he jumps," says Andrea, looking adoringly at Ben in his stall. "He's pretty, and he seems friendly. I thought he'd be mean."

Just then, three children approached Big Ben. The stall door was open: only a chain covered in blue plastic restrained the horse, so the children were free to pat him if he would agree to it. (He will even play catch with children, tossing them a brush by releasing it as he lifts his head in a bob. Sandi says he is a fine pitcher; catching, so far, is beyond him.)

This time he came forward and obligingly lowered his head for each child, but when adults drifted by they got the old ho-hum. Suddenly Big Ben was very interested in the stall floor or in trying to look over the wall at the horse next door.

In the big Saturday class at the Collingwood Horse Show, Big Ben went clear in the first round, and though he and Ian took down a rail in the jumpoff and thus incurred four faults, they were the fastest of the four-faulters and so took second place. It was a nice tune-up for the Spruce Meadows Masters in Calgary only a few weeks away.

What makes Big Ben such a brilliant horse? Mac Cone, a fine rider from Tennessee, has thought deeply about that question. At the Collingwood show, he sat on a tack box and offered his answer.

Mac's first instinct was to credit the horse's trainer. "Ian taught him to be clever and agile. That agility surprises me — his inside turns, his quickness. You would not expect he could do that. There are lots of big horses with power that jump like Big Ben or better, but they lack his agility. He's also got this great desire to win. It's special.

"And the nice thing about Ben is that he's been a hero for Canada. I've been to the Meadowlands in New Jersey, where the U.S. national competition is held. Big Ben is a Canadian horse but he gets the biggest applause of any horse there. He's known everywhere."

The days were long at the Collingwood Horse Show, and they began at dawn. By midnight, all was quiet on the grounds. Soft lights glowed in the horse tents and illuminated the green-and-white striped canvas. From above, the tents must have looked like giant lampshades. A lone police car slowly patrolled the grounds.

In his stall, "that one" as Harold Chopping called him, that prince of a horse called Ben, was resting.

Young fans admire Big Ben at the Collingwood Horse Show in 1993.
(Photos by Jayne Huddleston)

And if a fly were to land on his nose, the old prince might shake his head and shoo the fly himself. Or he might wish that Sandi or Grant would come along soon to do it for him.

12

When
the Show
Is Over

Though he is a senior horse who has seen and done much, and though he has mellowed in many ways, Big Ben is still easily spooked.

One day in the summer of 1993, when Big Ben was seventeen years old, a visitor observed him in his paddock. Sandi usually leans on the fence and keeps Big Ben company for these hour-long stays, and normally Future Vision is in the neighbouring paddock. But Sandi had been called away to a meeting of grooms and it was Baarlo next door today.

"Ben was fine," Dutch trainer Bert Romp had said almost a decade before, "as long as there were no surprises."

Quite suddenly, Ben began to neigh furiously. He cantered in mad circles, then reared and slammed his front hooves into the ground. He lashed out with his hind end. Sandi came running. Lynn came running. They took the agitated horse and walked him in circles around the gravel parking lot. In minutes, he had settled down. The storm had passed.

Lynn diagnosed the problem. "He must have suddenly realized that he was alone out there. And he got really upset."

At the age of seventeen, many horses, even the spirited ones, begin to wind down. But while he has grown a little more placid with his advancing years, Big Ben retains much of the fire that makes him such a champion in the show ring. It is still the rule with Ben that the more keyed up he is before a tournament, the more likely he is to win. Ian sometimes has too much horse under him. He never has too little.

On two occasions, Big Ben has thrown Ian to the ground. It has happened at competitions, most notably Spruce Meadows in Calgary. Ian remembers that time very well.

"I was out there on Big Ben, just before the parade," — a crowd-pleasing tradition at Spruce Meadows that features marching bands, floats, and skydiving. "A plane came over us," Ian continued, warming to his tale, "so low it had leaves in its landing gear." Ian paused to let the exaggeration hit home. "Big Ben spooked and threw me up to there," he pointed to a spot in the clouds, "and away went Ben galloping down a paved road, hooves flying." Ian called up the tale as he would an old nightmare. He can laugh about it now.

"When he throws me," Ian says, "Big Ben is telling me 'I'm big and strong and capable, and you are too. So let's play.' He doesn't know his own strength. There isn't a mean bone in his body."

Big Ben has always been a horse with a mind of his own. Once at Spruce Meadows, he had just won an event. After the usual victory gallop, Ian dismounted and Sandi led the horse towards the barn. Or tried to. Big Ben saw other horses and riders lining up for one of the many parades put on at Spruce Meadows and was determined to join them. Sandi had to practically drag him away.

Other days, parades visibly annoy him. During ribbon presentation ceremonies, Big Ben has aimed kicks at Pierre Durand's Jappeloup and Gail Greenough's Mr. T. "He only kicks the best horses," Sandi says. Once in Halifax, the horse drew laughter from the audience when he tried to kick the course designer — the person paid to trip the horses up.

Ian will continue to jump Big Ben as long as he senses that the enthusiasm is still there. "He'll tell us when he's ready to retire," Ian once said in a television interview, and then he added with a smile, "He hasn't mentioned it yet."

Ian knows well what makes the horse great. "He's brave brave brave. He's a straight shooter. He never lies to you. Some do. Horses can let you down. Ben never does. You always get his best. You combine his bravery with his generosity and the heart of a lion and you match that with his physical gifts, and you have Ben."

When Big Ben was sixteen, CBC-TV produced a short documentary on him and at the end of it Ian was heard to say with uncommon feeling and emotion, "He really is the wind beneath my wings." Ian's eyes filled up a little, the voice catching on the last word. Then the camera cut to a familiar scene shown in slow motion: Ian on Ben after yet another clear round, the rider slapping the horse's neck in elation, the backdrop a sea of clapping hands in the stands. The documentary ends with more slow-motion footage, this time showing Sandi leading Big Ben in a victory blanket to Ian, who has his arms spread wide in welcome, as if to a long-lost relative. Smiles all around. Then he leans over and kisses his horse on the neck.

The camera finally freezes on Big Ben, who turns sideways to look straight at the camera, straight at you.

★ ★ ★

(Photo by Jayne Huddleston)

When he does retire, Big Ben will spend more time in the paddock, *his* paddock, the one to the north of the barn. Perhaps he will learn in time to age gracefully, and not to whinny and complain when the Millar Brooke horse trailer heads down the lane without him. For Sandi and Ian, this has always been proof that the big guy loved his work and could not abide being left behind.

"This is what he loves doing," Sandi tells people. "Some horses like to eat. Some horses like to sleep. Big Ben likes to go out and jump."

Someone on the farm will ride him, keep him limber. It will not be Ian, for Ian will have other horses to ride and get ready for the ring. But will he ever ride one the likes of Big Ben? It seems unlikely. Ian will regret that, and yet he will always feel privileged to have had Big Ben as a partner. For a long, long time, they were magic together.

Sandi will keep her old horse well stocked with bran muffins. Bennie will scratch his nose on her back and nicker to her as she passes his paddock on her rounds. Sandi will always stop to pat him, and she will always remember him. You do not stop being pals with your best friend just because he quits his job.

And maybe on the odd Sunday afternoon, around grand prix time, something will click in the old chestnut gelding. He may pick up the canter and circle deep in one corner of the paddock. Maybe he will remember in his own way the ring, the banners, the cheers, the little buzz that ran through the crowd whenever his rider headed him to that first jump. We who saw Big Ben perform will remember that he vaulted fences with unsurpassed grace and power and speed. In the beginning, he surprised us. All his life, and in so many ways, he surprised us.

The wind may blow across his paddock and lift his mane. He will hold his head and tail high once more. The white socks will fly, just for a few seconds, and then the moment will pass, like that little tempest in the paddock during the summer of '93. The great horse, the one with scars over his eye and along his belly who touched us in ways we barely understand, will ease up, lower his head and go back to his richly deserved feed of grass.

A Brief Chronology

1976
- the colt named Winston is born on April 20 in Belgium

1978
- Winston jumps his first fence

1983
- Winston excels in early competitions
- Winston is sold to a Dutch trainer and renamed Big Ben
- Ian Millar buys Big Ben and takes him to Canada

1984
- Big Ben comes second at his first grand prix, in Edmonton
- competes in L.A. Olympics and earns a team 4th

1986
- wins his first derby at Spruce Meadows, Calgary
- comes second at World Cup in Gothenburg, Sweden

1987
- Sandi Patterson becomes a groom at Millar Brooke Farm
- Big Ben wins two golds at the Pan American Games
- wins the prestigious Masters grand prix at Spruce Meadows

1988
- wins the World Cup at Gothenburg
- comes a disappointing 15th in the Seoul Olympics

1989
- wins second consecutive World Cup in Tampa, Florida
- wins the grand prix at Stuttgart, W. Germany
- wins the grand prix of Bordeaux, France
- returns to Belgium a hero

1990
- suffers his first attack of colic
- recovers and is named Canadian champion

1991
- felled by colic a second time
- once again wins the Spruce Meadows Masters grand prix

1992
- survives a terrible highway accident
- wins the grand prix at Spruce Meadows two weeks later
- finishes badly at the Barcelona Olympics

1993
- wins the Spruce Meadows derby for the 6th time